No Lack

*Principles For Unleashing God's
Unlimited Abundance In Your Life*

By Dr. Preston T. Adams, III

Copyright ©2016 Preston T. Adams, III
Indianapolis, Indiana USA

Unless otherwise indicated, all Scripture quotations are taken from the King James Version of The Holy Bible. Also taken from The Holy Bible, English Standard Version® (ESV®) Copyright © 2001 by Crossway, a publishing ministry of Good News Publishers.

Your purchase of the *No Lack, Only Provision: Principles For Unleashing God's Unlimited Abundance In Your Life* is for your own personal use. You may not copy it, either for resale or to give away to others. Making copies, either for resale or to give away, is a violation of United States copyright law.

According to the United States Copyright Office, "Copyright infringement occurs when a copyrighted work is reproduced, distributed, performed, publicly displayed, or made into a derivative work without the permission of the copyright owner." For further information, please see: http://ww.copyright.gov/help/faq/faq-definitions.html

Cover Design by CreativeChurch Marketing Solutions
www.creativechurchmarketing.org
Cover Design Idea by Lady Greta E. Adams

Publication production provided by Vision Communications
www.VisioncomSolutions.com

PUBLISHED BY
PTA Ministries, Inc.
www.prestonadams.com
www.comemeetgrace.org

Contents

Dedication

Forward

Introduction — 7

1 | The Principle Of Dominion — 11

2 | The Principle Of Seed Time and Harvest — 19

3 | The Principle Of Departure — 25

4 | The Principle of Fearlessness — 33

5 | The Principle of Favor — 39

6 | The Principle of Faith — 45

7 | The Principle of Sowing and Reaping — 51

8 | The Principle of Generational Wealth — 61

9 | Conclusion — 73

10 | 30 Days of No Lack, Only Provision Affirmations — 75

11 | No Lack, Only Provision Scriptures — 91

12 | Supporting Quotes — 101

No Lack Only Provision Journal Pages — 107

Bibliography/Additional Resources — 115

About The Author — 116

Dedication

To our first granddaughter, Zara Macai, my "Zara Boo." Your entry into our world gave me a new vision for life and opened my eyes even more to God's amazing promise of *No Lack, Only Provision.*

Forward

This book spoke to me. God is using you my brother in a mighty way. I do not know what your whole purpose was in writing this book. I do know that it causes one to reinforce their faith in the Word that God has given us. It causes one to self-examine your life and how one is walking in relation to the Lord's plan for us. It also makes you tighten up your determination and outlook on life.

Dr. Adams, your writing reveals aspects of the Lord's plan that many believers do not understand or aren't aware of. This book preaches as well as it teaches. This book strengthens God's Kingdom and empowers His people.

Keep proclaiming the Gospel. Your God inspired writing, backed by scripture, moves believers in Christ to become Kingdom builders. Blessed be the Lord who inspires you to inspire His church.

Your Little Brother,

Delrick B. Adams

 # Introduction

Genesis 8:22 – *"While the earth remains, seedtime and harvest, cold and heat, summer and winter, and day and night shall not cease."*

"If you use these principles wisely and intelligently, there can be no uncertainty as to the outcome of any endeavor, and not limit [no lack] to your possibilities [only provision]." – John McDonald, The Message of a Master

The purpose of this book is to revolutionize your thinking and actions regarding God's unlimited provisions, which are available to all of God's people. It is written with the intent of teaching the reader how to unleash God's unlimited abundance in your life. The good news of both the Old and New Testament writings is that God is present in our existence continuously. We don't have to wait until the "hereafter," next life, or heaven (for those of us who are follows of the Christian faith) to experience God's fullness. We can have access to, and enjoy, all of God's abundance right here and right now.

The central theme: "There is no lack, only provision," came as the result of my spending time with God in prayer and meditation during a season when my own personal provisions were at an all time low. I had recently left a long-term executive pastorate at a large congregation to plant a new church. You might be saying *"Ok, I know of people who have done that so what makes your situation unique?"* I was 50 years old at the time and had served in my previous congregation for over 20 years, the last seven as its Executive Pastor and second in command. Most people thought I would be that congregation's next Senior Pastor because of my longevity and faithfulness. But God had other plans for my family and me. At a time when most 50 year olds are planning for retirement in the next 10-15 years, God told me to *"Get thee out of thy father's house and go to a land I will show you."* (Genesis 12:1)

As I was praying for God to unleash resources in my life during a new church pastor's conference in California, God spoke directly to me. Interestingly enough, my hotel room was right on the ocean, with the shore less than 200 yards away from my door. It was nighttime and I could hear the waves crashing upon the shore. God told me to go and stand outside of my door and just listen. When I got outside, God spoke to me and said *"My son, do you see how the waves continue to come ashore? They haven't stopped and they won't ever stop as long as the earth remains. That's how my provision is for you and all of my children. As long as the earth remains, my provision will never stop. Don't worry my son, just remember, there is no lack, only provision."*

From that moment on I began to speak those words: "There is no lack, only provision." I would speak these words in the morning, afternoon, evening, and every time I felt like I needed reassurance that God had me covered. And, what began to happen next is phenomenal. Unlimited resources started flowing my way. Every area of my life became flooded with everything I needed and more. I began to post the mantra on Facebook and Twitter along with testimonies of God's goodness and abundance. Others began to pick up the mantra and they too starting receiving God's unlimited abundance. What began as a mantra morphed into a movement! No Lack, Only Provision became real.

It was at this point that God spoke to me again and said, *"The mantra I gave you needs to be taught in my church where you pastor. Teach the people of Amazing Grace Christian Church principles of provision around the mantra. As I give you the principles, you teach them. As you teach them, I will bless you and my people with unlimited abundance."*

This book contains those principles. There are eight total and they are powerful and promise to unleash God abundance when applied practically in your life. These principles are: (1) The Principle of Dominion; (2) The Principle of Seed Time and Harvest; (3) The Principle of Departure; (4) The Principle of Fearlessness; (5) The Principle of Favor; (6) The Principle of Faith; (7) The Principle of Sowing and Reaping; and (8) The Principle of Generational Wealth.

Let's explore the Principles Of Provision. I promise, you'll never think or experience lack again!

No Lack, Only Provision!

CHAPTER ONE

The Principle of Dominion

Genesis 1:26-28

²⁶ And God said, Let us make man in our image, after our likeness: and let them have dominion over the fish of the sea, and over the fowl of the air, and over the cattle, and over all the earth, and over every creeping thing that creepeth upon the earth.

²⁷ So God created man in his own image, in the image of God created he him; male and female created he them.

²⁸ And God blessed them, and God said unto them, Be fruitful, and multiply, and replenish the earth, and subdue it: and have dominion over the fish of the sea, and over the fowl of the air, and over every living thing that moveth upon the earth.

Ephesian 1:15-23

¹⁵ Wherefore I also, after I heard of your faith in the Lord Jesus, and love unto all the saints,

¹⁶ Cease not to give thanks for you, making mention of you in my prayers;

¹⁷ That the God of our Lord Jesus Christ, the Father of

glory, may give unto you the spirit of wisdom and revelation in the knowledge of him:

18 The eyes of your understanding being enlightened; that ye may know what is the hope of his calling, and what the riches of the glory of his inheritance in the saints,

19 And what is the exceeding greatness of his power to us-ward who believe, according to the working of his mighty power,

20 Which he wrought in Christ, when he raised him from the dead, and set him at his own right hand in the heavenly places,

21 Far above all principality, and power, and might, and dominion, and every name that is named, not only in this world, but also in that which is to come:

22 And hath put all things under his feet, and gave him to be the head over all things to the church, 23 Which is his body, the fulness of him that filleth all in all.

"I am the master of my own destiny, and I can make my life anything that I wish it to be." – John McDonald, The Message of a Master

The first, and one of the most critical, principles of provision to grasp is the Principle of Dominion. It is foundationally important that we understand and have complete confidence in the fact that God created us to have dominion. We were not created to be subdued. We were created to subdue. We were not created to be the tail. We were created to be the head. We were not created to be beneath. We were created to be above.

Too many people, especially Christians, live their lives in a state of lack. God never intended for us to live in lack. God created us to live in abundance and to have more than we need. Moving in abundance requires that we comprehend and apply the Principle of Dominion on a daily basis.

Webster's Dictionary defines dominion as *"control or power over, or the authority to rule."* It is sovereignty. Dominion implies more power than that — even absolute power. A dominion can also be an area or territory controlled by a larger country or state. Here are some interesting quotes I found on dominion:

> *"Satan cannot win. Why not? Because he has denied God's sovereignty and disobeyed God's law. But Moses was told explicitly, God's blessings come only from obedience. Satan will not win because he has abandoned God's tool of dominion, biblical law."*
>
> Gary North
>
> *"Your real self - the 'I am I' - is master of this land, the ruler of this empire. You rightfully have power and dominion over it, all its inhabitants, and all contained in its realm."*
>
> Robert Collier

The Bible speaks about dominion and more importantly, about the dominion God has granted to every believer.

> *"For sin will have no dominion over you, since you are not under law but under grace."* Romans 6:14 (ESV)
>
> *"Behold, I have given you authority to tread on serpents and scorpions, and over all the power of the enemy, and nothing shall hurt you."* Luke 10:19 (ESV)

Make no mistake about it, dominion is in the DNA of every child of God. This truth is initially established in Genesis 1:26-28:

> ²⁶ *And God said, Let us make man in our image, after our likeness: and let them have dominion over the fish of the sea, and over the fowl of the air, and over the cattle, and over all the earth, and over every creeping thing that creepeth upon the earth.*
>
> ²⁷ *So God created man in his own image, in the image of God created he him; male and female created he them.*
>
> ²⁸ *And God blessed them, and God said unto them, Be fruitful, and multiply, and replenish the earth, and subdue it: and have dominion over the fish of the sea, and over the fowl of the air, and over every living thing that moveth upon the earth.*

We are created in God's image – the Imago Dei. *Imago Dei*, Latin for "*the image of God*" refers to the way the God of the Bible created people. We are created to subdue the earth. We are created with dominion. Ephesians 2:1-8 further confirms this point:

1 And you hath he quickened, who were dead in trespasses and sins;

2 Wherein in time past ye walked according to the course of this world, according to the prince of the power of the air, the spirit that now worketh in the children of disobedience:

3 Among whom also we all had our conversation in times past in the lusts of our flesh, fulfilling the desires of the flesh and of the mind; and were by nature the children of wrath, even as others.

4 But God, who is rich in mercy, for his great love wherewith he loved us,

5 Even when we were dead in sins, hath quickened us together with Christ, (by grace ye are saved;)

6 And hath raised us up together, and made us sit together in heavenly places in Christ Jesus:

7 That in the ages to come he might shew the exceeding riches of his grace in his kindness toward us through Christ Jesus.

8 For by grace are ye saved through faith; and that not of yourselves: it is the gift of God:

We are born into a sinful nature. But God works on our behalf, through the power of the Holy Spirit, to eventually call us out of sin and darkness and into God's marvelous light. The sending of God's Son, Jesus Christ, and the Kingdom work Christ did while here on earth became the catalyst and propitiation for our redemption. Christ sacrifice on Calvary's cross, His death, burial, and subsequent resurrection, became the bridge for us to be reconciled with God. God called us out and we have been raised up with Christ. We are saved by grace through faith. This is the DNA that exists in all of us who are God's children and believers in Jesus Christ.

Dominion does not discriminate. Jeremiah 12:1 notes the following: *"Righteous art thou, O LORD, when I plead with thee: yet let me talk with thee of thy judgments: Wherefore doth the way of the wicked prosper? wherefore are all they happy that deal very treacherously?"* Psalm 73:3 states: *"For I was envious at the foolish, When I saw the prosperity of the wicked."* And, why do the wicked prosper? It's simple: dominion does not discriminate. And if the wicked exercise dominion in the earth and prosper, albeit for a season before judgment comes, how much more should we who are God's children...God's elect and chosen prosper? As Delrick Adams notes: *"Besides John 3:16, Ephesians 1:8 shows the Lord's infinite concern and love for us. He [God] has given us everything. Still the Lord continues to give us even more."*

Dominion must be exercised. It cannot just be possessed. An inherent dominion that is not exercised is like a car with a powerful engine and a tank full of gas that is never driven. That vehicle is little more than a show car. Believers who don't exercise dominion are nothing more than show pieces in the Kingdom. But God desires more of us than just show. We are not to function as trophies sitting on a shelf. We are to exercise the dominion that's intricately woven into our DNA.

Here's what Genesis 2:19-20 says: "*19 And out of the ground the LORD God formed every beast of the field, and every fowl of the air; and brought them unto Adam to see what he would call them: and whatsoever Adam called every living creature, that was the name thereof. 20 And Adam gave names to all cattle, and to the fowl of the air, and to every beast of the field; but for Adam there was not found an help meet for him.*"

Dominion had to be exercised. God gave dominion to Adam, but Adam needed to exercise what God had given him. So God put Adam in position to exercise his dominion when he placed him in authority over the Garden. What position has God placed us in? Ephesians 1:15-23 tells us:

15 Wherefore I also, after I heard of your faith in the Lord Jesus, and love unto all the saints,

16 Cease not to give thanks for you, making mention of you in my prayers;

17 That the God of our Lord Jesus Christ, the Father of glory, may give unto you the spirit of wisdom and revelation in the knowledge of him:

18 The eyes of your understanding being enlightened; that ye may know what is the hope of his calling, and what the riches of the glory of his inheritance in the saints,

19 And what is the exceeding greatness of his power to

us-ward who believe, according to the working of his mighty power,

²⁰ Which he wrought in Christ, when he raised him from the dead, and set him at his own right hand in the heavenly places,

²¹ Far above all principality, and power, and might, and dominion, and every name that is named, not only in this world, but also in that which is to come:

²² And hath put all things under his feet, and gave him to be the head over all things to the church,

²³ Which is his body, the fulness of him that filleth all in all.

Christ is far above and we have been raised up with Him. Ephesians 2:6 further states: *"And hath raised us up together, and made us sit together in heavenly places in Christ Jesus:"* Adam was given dominion and we have that same dominion! The Principle of Dominion is in the DNA of every child of God, dominion does not discriminate, and dominion must be exercised.

CHAPTER TWO
The Principle of Seed Time and Harvest

Genesis 8:22 -- *While the earth remaineth, seedtime and harvest, and cold and heat, and summer and winter, and day and night shall not cease.*

"If what you have in your hand is not what you need, then what you have in your hand must be your seed." -- Anonymous

Seedtime and harvest is a divine and eternal system that God has set in place for the purpose of insuring that everything reproduces after its own kind. Seed is the means of propagating life from one generation to another, whether plant, animal, or human. Growth in any life form begins with a seed. Our knowledge base, intuitions, aspirations, achievements, natural or spiritual, begin with a seed.

Seed is used for eating. Genesis 1:29 notes: *"And God said, Behold, I have given you every herb bearing seed, which is upon the face of all the earth, and every tree, in the which is the fruit of a tree yielding seed; to you it shall be for meat."* Seed is used as an offering. 2

Chronicles 31:5 says: *"And as soon as the commandment came abroad, the children of Israel brought in abundance the Firstfruits of corn, wine, and oil, and honey, and of all the increase of the field; and the tithe of all things brought they in abundantly."*

The presence of seed is considered a blessing. The Prophet Zechariah notes in Zechariah 8:12: *"For the seed shall be prosperous; the vine shall give her fruit, and the ground shall give her increase, and the heavens shall give their dew; and I will cause the remnant of this people to possess all these things."*

The absence of seed was considered a curse. Look at what Joel 1:16-17 states: *"16 Is not the meat cut off before our eyes, Yea, joy and gladness from the house of our God? 17 The seed is rotten under their clods, The garners are laid desolate, the barns are broken down; For the corn is withered."*

Seed is meant to be harvested. Harvest is the gathering of mature crops from the land. It is the successful culmination of the agricultural year and was evidence of God's goodness and consequently marked with festivity. Harvest is evidence of God's goodness according to Psalm 85:12 – *"12 Yea, the LORD shall give that which is good; And our land shall yield her increase.* Leviticus 26:9-10 - 9 further declares: *"For I will be leaning toward you with favor and regard for you, rendering you fruitful, multiplying you, and establishing and ratifying My covenant with you. 10 And you shall eat the [abundant] old store of produce long kept, and clear out the old [to make room] for the new."* (AMP)

Seedtime and harvest is a system God has set in place, and it's a system designed to last as long as the earth remains. Genesis 8:22 is a passage of scripture the follows the story of the flood. According to the biblical narrative, God had destroyed the earth by water, saving only Noah and his wife and his sons and their wives. Every species was also spared in twos, giving every species the ability to reproduces after its own kind.

In Genesis 8:21, God promised that He would never again curse the ground because of the evil in the human heart. While the earth remains, God's word says, *"... seedtime and harvest, cold and heat, summer and winter, night and day shall not cease."* Based on God's promise, here are some questions for us to consider: *"How do I implement or build on the Principle of Seedtime and Harvest?" "What Is Sowing With A Purpose?" "Where Is My Harvest?"*

First and foremost, examine the seeds you are currently planting. Let's look at a few pivotal scriptures regarding seeds and sowing:

Proverbs 11:18 *"The wicked man earns deceitful wages, but he who sows righteousness (moral and spiritual rectitude in every area and relation) shall have a sure reward [permanent and satisfying]."*

Hosea 8:7 *"For they sow the wind and they shall reap the whirlwind. The standing grain has no heads; it shall yield no meal; if it were to yield, strangers and aliens would eat it up."*

Galatians 6:7 *"Do not be deceived and deluded and

misled; God will not allow Himself to be sneered at (scorned, disdained, or mocked [a]by mere pretensions or professions, or by His precepts being set aside.) [He inevitably deludes himself who attempts to delude God.] For whatever a man sows, that and [b]that only is what he will reap."

Secondly, plant the seeds for the type of harvest you want to grow. Once again, we find wisdom and instruction in the scriptures.

Genesis 1:11 "And God said, Let the earth put forth [tender] vegetation: plants yielding seed and fruit trees yielding fruit whose seed is in itself, each according to its kind, upon the earth. And it was so."

God has given every species, every plant, and every reproducing entity the power to continue replenishing the earth according to its own kind. This is the greatest example of seedtime and harvest. But too many of us miss our harvest because we don't sow abundantly. Look at 2 Corinthians 9:6 "[Remember] this: he who sows sparingly and grudgingly will also reap sparingly and grudgingly, and he who sows generously [[a]that blessings may come to someone] will also reap generously and with blessings." Don't miss your harvest! Don't miss the opportunity to reap bountiful blessing because you either don't sow or you sow sparingly.

The harvest is waiting for you. John 4:35 says; "Do you not say, It is still four months until harvest time comes? Look! I tell you, raise your eyes and observe the fields *and see how they are already white for harvesting."*

God's covenant regarding seedtime and harvest, sowing and reaping is indeed an eternal covenant. Jeremiah 33:20-21 reminds us; *"Thus says the Lord: If you can break My covenant with the day, and My covenant with the night, so that there should not be day and night in their season, Then can also My covenant be broken with David My servant, so that he shall not have a son to reign upon his throne, and [My league be broken also] with the Levitical priests, My ministers."*

There is unlimited power in God's covenant promises. While human promises are often broken, and some even believe promises are made to be broken, God's covenant promises are solemn and can be counted on.

Seedtime and harvest is a covenant promise! Think about this: Jesus Christ, our Lord and Savior, was a seed. He was a seed sown 42 generations before He manifested in the earth - Matthew 1:17 – *"So all the generations from Abraham to David are fourteen, from David to the Babylonian exile (deportation) fourteen generations, from the Babylonian exile to the Christ fourteen generations."* He is the Son (seed) of David and the Son (seed) of Abraham. He was sown into the earth that we might be reconciled back to God. A seed that was planted before the foundation of the world, germinated and manifested in the earth, and continues to produce fruit (souls) after its own kind to this present day. Why? It's the Principle of Seedtime and Harvest in full effect!

The Principle of Seed Time and Harvest is God's eternal plan and God's eternal promise. We must believe God for seed to sow. We must sow generously in faith and trust completely God's will to manifest harvest. We must believe God to meet our every need while the seed grows. We must believe God to multiply the seed sown. And, we must believe God for a generous harvest.

CHAPTER THREE

The Principle of Departure

Genesis 12:1-4

¹ Now [in Haran] the Lord said to Abram, Go for yourself [for your own advantage] away from your country, from your relatives and your father's house, to the land that I will show you.

² And I will make of you a great nation, and I will bless you [with abundant increase of favors] and make your name famous and distinguished, and you will be a blessing [dispensing good to others].

³ And I will bless those who bless you [who confer prosperity or happiness upon you] and [a] curse him who curses or uses insolent language toward you; in you will all the families and kindred of the earth be blessed [and by you they will bless themselves].

⁴ So Abram departed, as the Lord had directed him; and Lot [his nephew] went with him. Abram was seventy-five years old when he left Haran. (AMP)

"Some of these mornings and it won't be long, you gonna wake up calling me and I'll be gone." -- Blues

In this chapter I want to explore a pivotal and important principle that could easily be misinterpreted or even overlooked totally. Let's spend some time digging into The Principle of Departure.

Webster defines departure as the act of leaving. Departure is a starting out, as on a trip or a new course of action. It is a divergence or deviation, as from an established rule, plan, or procedure. The Principle of Departure simply stated means one must be willing to leave their current space in order to get their new place. Departure means leaving the familiar and venturing out into the unfamiliar. Understanding the Principle of Departure means also understanding why remaining in the same space can block our blessings.

So what is the same space? For some it's working the same job even though there is no opportunity for advancement or further fulfillment beyond a paycheck and the appearance of job security. For others, it's living in the same house, same neighborhood, and same city most or all of their life. And for others it may be the same relationships with the same people that we should have broken away from. It could even be the same church. The church we grew up in may have been the church for our parents and grandparents, but it may not be the church for us.

Please don't take offense to any of the above scenarios or miss the message I'm seeking to convey by misinterpreting my thought process. There's absolutely nothing wrong with being the kind of person that functions best in a settled (same) location, job, relationship, or church for the long haul. But there is something wrong with knowing God has called us to leave the familiar and missing our blessings because we fail to flow in the Principle of Departure.

Let's face a stark reality: sometimes God call us to depart. God calls us to move or separate from that which is familiar and venture into the unfamiliar. So why won't we depart? Is it a mistrust of God? Mistrust of ourselves? Lack of confidence? It could be either of those factors. But often it is simply fear of the unknown. Think about it this way, we are largely creatures of habit. We eat the same foods, travel to work on the same route, wear the same brand of clothes, comb our hair in the same style, frequent the same places of business, and have regular conversations with many of the same people. It's all a part of our normal daily routine. So the prospect of departing from any, most, or sometimes, all of our routines can invoke fears and insecurity due to uncertainty.

But our faith must override our fear. When we start to experience fear, we must remind ourselves that we have been created in the Imago Dei or the image of God. Some of our greatest minds provide some awesome insights:

Minister Jason Powell

> "God lives in you and He is ever declaring and decreeing in you, through you, and as you!"

Joel Osteen

"I declare I will experience God's faithfulness. I will not worry. I will not doubt. I will keep my trust in Him knowing that He will not fail me."

Tennessee Williams

"There is a time for departure even when there is nowhere to go."

Tori Amos

"Sometimes you have to take a departure from what you do regularly in order to get inspiration."

Abram is told in Genesis 12 that he has to leave and go. He has to leave three things: His country, his people, and his father's household. These are the very things that would give anyone of us a sense of security. But Abram is told to leave them. Notice that Abram is not told specifically where to go. But he is told that his destination will be his inheritance from the Lord. He need not have fear or anxiety about where he will end up, for the Lord's presence will be there for him.

If God has spoken to you and told you to leave the familiar for the unfamiliar, why have you not departed? What are you afraid of? Why do you fear following the Lord's voice and command? If you are wrestling with some or all of these questions now would be a good time to grasp how you can apply the Principle of Departure. Here's the strategy.

First, be willing to leave all to go along with God. Genesis 19:17 notes the following: *"And when they had brought them forth, they said, Escape for your life! Do not look behind you or stop anywhere in [a]the whole valley; escape to the mountains [of Moab], lest you be consumed."* Sometimes we must literally escape for our lives. The situation we find ourselves in may be one of stagnation or even worse it may be toxic. In order to live we must escape and not look back or let anything stop us from departing.

Wisdom is a needed ingredient in the Principle of Departure. Proverbs 9:12 says; *"If you are wise, you are wise for yourself; if you scorn, you alone will bear it and pay the penalty."* Jesus makes it clear that in order for us to follow Him, we must also depart leaving family, friends, and maybe even our own children behind as we go. Luke 14:26 is considered one of the "Hard Sayings Of Jesus" – *"If anyone comes to Me and does not hate his [own] father and mother [[a]in the sense of indifference to or relative disregard for them in comparison with his attitude toward God] and [likewise] his wife and children and brothers and sisters—[yes] and even his own life also—he cannot be My disciple."*

We glean this from Matthew Henry's Commentary Notes: *"Natural affection must give way to divine grace. Our country is dear to us, our kindred dearer, and our father's house dearest of all; And yet they must all be hated (Luke 14:26), that is, we must love them less than Christ, hate them in comparison with him,*

And, whenever any of these come in competition with him, they must be postponed, and the preference given to the will and honour of the Lord Jesus

We must be willing to trust God further than we can see God."

Second, resist the urge to remain comfortable, or stay in your "comfort zone," when you know God is telling you it's time to go. The comfort zone is a behavioral state within which a person operates in an anxiety-neutral condition. The comfort zone uses a limited set of behaviors to deliver a steady level of performance, usually without a sense of risk. Alasdair A. K. White notes that his or her comfort zones can describe a person's personality. A comfort zone is a type of mental conditioning that causes a person to create and operate mental boundaries. Such boundaries create an unfounded sense of security.

Like inertia, a person who has established a comfort zone in a particular axis of his or her life, will tend to stay within that zone without stepping outside of it. To step outside their comfort zone, a person must experiment with new and different behaviors, and then experience the new and different responses that occur within their environment.

Do you see where this is going? Abram had to step out of his comfort zone. So Abram departed and received these six promises from God:

1. I will make of thee a great nation (Genesis 12:2)

2. I will bless thee (Genesis 12:2)
3. I will make thy name great (Genesis 12:2)
4. Thou shalt be a blessing (Genesis 12:2)
5. I will bless them that bless thee and curseth him that curse thee
6. In thee shall all the families of the earth be blessed

Abram had to depart Ur in order to receive God's promises. Because of Abram's obedience, God changed his name to Abraham, made him the father of many nations, blessed him supernaturally, and even extended the blessings to all of his generations, to include us. Yes, Abraham's obedience was the ultimate blessing for you and me.

Jesus had to depart as well. He had to depart heaven and come to earth wrapped in humanity. He had to depart His place of birth, His family, and even some of His customs to preach about the coming kingdom or realm of God being manifested in the earth. Ultimately, He would have to depart this earthly realm by way of an old rugged cross on a hill called Calvary. His departure would lead Him through a borrowed tomb, a glorious resurrection with all power given to Him, and back to His rightful place sitting on the right hand of God the Father with all things under His feet.

If Abraham had to depart to receive his promises, and Jesus had to depart to fulfill prophecy and receive the promises made to Him, we too must be ready and willing to employ The Principle of Departure.

The Principle Of Departure. Where is God telling you to go? What land is He telling you to leave behind? Where have you overstayed your welcome? Be willing to go where God takes you. Be willing to go further than God allows you to see. Be obedient to God's command.

CHAPTER FOUR
The Principle of Fearlessness

Genesis 15:1

1 After these things the word of the LORD came unto Abram in a vision, saying, Fear not, Abram: I am thy shield, and thy exceeding great reward.

"I am the master of my own destiny, and I can make my life anything I wish it to be." – John McDonald, "The Message of a Master"

"Fear is the path to the dark side" -Yoda

To this point in my work, I've introduced you to The Principle of Dominion, The Principle of Seedtime and Harvest, and the Principle of Departure. Now, I want to explore the fourth principle: The Principle of Fearlessness.

Fearlessness is the quality of mind enabling one to face danger or hardship resolutely. Fearlessness is bravery, courage, dauntlessness, fortitude, or gallantry. A person or species that has heart would be considered fearless or game. It is intrepidness, spirit or stoutheartedness. To be fearless is to be valiant, have guts, or be willing to display gutsiness. In fact a popular phrase that used to describe fearlessness is "*No guts, no glory!*"

Internationally known motivational speaker Les Brown says this about being fearless: "*Make your move before you're ready. Kick your fears, excuses and procrastination to the curb. Stop giving yourself reasons for standing still, failing to act and playing it safe!*"

Fearlessness requires you to leap over your comfort zone and decide to live a life beyond survival. Let's take a moment and explore the comfort zone since breaking through it is so vital to walking in the Principle of Fearlessness.

The comfort zone "*is a psychological state in which a person feels familiar, at ease, in control and experiences low anxiety and stress. In the zone a steady level of performance is possible.*" (Source: Wikipedia)

Judith M. Bardwick defines the term as "*a behavioral state where a person operates in an anxiety-neutral position.*" Professor Brene Brown describes it as "*Where our uncertainty, scarcity and vulnerability are minimized — where we believe we'll have access to enough love, food, talent, time, admiration. Where we feel we have some control.*"

Evelyn Baker notes "*life begins at the end of your comfort zone.*" Baker also says: "*If given the opportunity to do something new or hard, do it. People are adaptable *creatures, meant to withstand difficulties and grow from them."* A famous Zen saying goes like this: *"Leap and the net will appear."*

The comfort zone can be your worst enemy. Things may happen to you that you can't anticipate. But you must learn to roll with the punches and keep moving because you have what it takes to get through any challenge in life.

Referring again to Matthew Henry's Commentary we find some instructive notes on Genesis 13. Henry helps us understand that this passage of scripture comes after a time of great victory for Abram. He has defeated four kings in war and saved his loved ones from danger. God comes to him in a vision to show him favor because he had shown favor to those in distress. God also comes to Abram in a vision and imparts upon him a divine revelation. Abram is given a gracious assurance of God's favor to him.

God calls him by name—*Abram*. This was a great honor to him because it is a fulfillment of God's promise found in Genesis 12 – *"I will make your name great."* It also provided Abram with great encouragement. This made his name great, provided great encouragement and was of great assistance to Abram's faith walk.

Has God called your name? What promises has God given to you? How should we respond to God's divine revelation? The only proper response is to fear not. Here's why:

Deuteronomy 11:24-26

24 Every place whereon the soles of your feet shall tread shall be yours: from the wilderness and Lebanon, from the river, the river Euphrates, even unto the uttermost sea shall your coast be.

*25 There shall no man be able to stand before you: for the L*ORD *your God shall lay the fear of you and the dread of you upon all the land that ye shall tread upon, as he hath said unto you.*

Psalm 27:1-3

*The L*ORD *is my light and my salvation; whom shall I fear? The L*ORD *is the strength of my life; of whom shall I be afraid? When the wicked, even mine enemies and my foes, came upon me to eat up my flesh, They stumbled and fell. Though an host should encamp against me, my heart shall not fear: Though war should rise against me, in this will I be confident.*

Fear not...everywhere we tread is ours. Fear not...no one will be able to stand against us. Fear Not...God will place fear upon our enemies. They will stumble and fall. Our hearts will be discontent at time. Wars will rise. But our position must always be Fear NOT!

Psalm 84:11 reminds us that *"The Lord God is a sun and shield."* A shield is an armament, security, guard, protection, safeguard or defense. Therefore, we have absolutely nothing to fear. And God withholds no good thing for those who walk uprightly. The Lord is our Great

Reward as Genesis 15:1 reminds us: *"After these things the word of the* LORD *came unto Abram in a vision, saying, Fear not, Abram: I am thy shield, and thy exceeding great reward."*

The Lord is our *"exceeding great reward."* In essence in the Lord we have been promised much abundance or very much in wages or payment. What a wonderful promise. What an awesome confirmation of No Lack, Only Provision!

The Principle Of Fearlessness. Fear Not. The Lord is our Shield. The Lord is our Great Reward. Les Brown exhorts us to *"Stay focused, determined, and positive."* You have something special. You have greatness within you. Decide today that you will walk in The Principle of Fearlessness.

No Lack, Only Provision!

CHAPTER FIVE
The Principle of Favor

Exodus 3:20-21

"*And I will stretch out my hand, and smite Egypt with all my wonders which I will do in the midst thereof: and after that he will let you go. And I will give this people favour in the sight of the Egyptians: and it shall come to pass, that, when ye go, ye shall not go empty.*"

"*I operate according to a definite, unwavering law… I know the outcome before I start.*" – John McDonald, The Message of a Master

    Favor is friendly regard shown toward another especially by a superior. It is an approving consideration or attention. Favor is gracious kindness or an act of such kindness. Favor manifests itself often in an effort in one's behalf or interest. Favor can also be considered a special privilege or right granted or conceded. Every one of us has God's favor. Acts 10:34 states: "*Then Peter opened his mouth, and said, of a truth I perceive that God is no respecter of persons:*" In essence, God does not favor anyone of us over the other. Every one of us is God's favorite!

This is important for us to grasp because if we are not careful, we can actually believe that God favors one person more than another. Have you ever felt like everyone else is getting ahead while you remain stagnant? Or, others seem to get breaks in life that you don't get? Do you believe that people who are born into certain families, specifically families with money, celebrity ties, or networks have a better chance at succeeding and reaching their goals than you do? If you answered, *"Yes"* to any of those questions then what you really saying is God shows favoritism to one person over another. But God's Word tells us just the opposite. God is indeed no respecter of persons!

Let's take a look at the story of Moses and the Children of Israel as a way of further expounding upon how God shows favor to all of God's people. Exodus chapter three begins with the story of the bush burning that would not be consumed. This burning bush was used to get Moses' attention because God had an assignment for him. God tells Moses that He is going to use him to deliver the Children of Israel from bondage. God has heard their moans and cries from the weight of over 400 years of oppression. And now it's time for their travail to end and for them to experience God's favor.

Moses makes a request of Pharaoh that he allow the Children of Israel to go into the desert for three days to offer sacrifices to God. Moses expected Pharaoh to resist this request but that doesn't deter him from making his request known. And not only does he make it known, he states it with confidence. God will act in power to demonstrate His sovereignty over Pharaoh and the Egyptians through judgments and miracles. God will further demonstrate His supremacy by ensuring that the eventually the Egyptians will favorably release the Egyptians. The Children of Israel would leave, but they would not leave empty-handed. Not only will the Egyptians allow them to go, they will equip them for the exodus by giving them articles of silver, gold, and clothing.

What do you need to understand about God's favor on your life? How should you handle God's favor? How long does God's favor last?

First of all, you must understand and accept the fact that favor isn't fair. What do I mean by this? Let's look at Exodus 12:36; *"And the LORD gave the people favour in the sight of the Egyptians, so that they lent unto them such things as they required. And they spoiled the Egyptians."* Favor in this context is adornment, charm, that which is pleasing or pleases. Favor is graciousness and favor comes when we ask, interrogate, consult, claim, demand, or wish.

Thus, it was mandatory for the Egyptians to give the Children of Israel everything they departed with. Why? They had God's favor on their lives and favor isn't fair. Some might argue that it wasn't fair for Egyptians to have to give of their riches to the Children of Israel. But favor, the favor God exhibits toward God's people isn't fair. God rewarded 400 years of bondage and suffering as we see in Exodus 12:36 – *"And the LORD had given the people favor in the sight of the Egyptians, so that they let them have what they asked. Thus they plundered the Egyptians."* Do you see what I see in this scripture? The Lord gave the people favor, they got everything they asked for, and what they received amounted to a *"plunder"*!

Secondly, while favor isn't fair, it also isn't free. In other words favor cost something. Not in monetary terms, in spiritual terms. Luke 12:48 states; *"But he that knew not, and did commit things worthy of stripes, shall be beaten with few stripes. For unto whomsoever much is given, of him shall be much required: and to whom men have committed much, of him they will ask the more."* Jesus died on Calvary for the favor of God that has been extended to us. It cost Jesus His life, which He freely gave. The scripture also tells us *"...unto whomsoever much is given, of him shall be much required."* You and I don't simply get to enjoy God's favor in abundance without a cost. We are required [mandated] of God to give back just as much or even more.

But what is much? Much is eminently, exceedingly, exceptionally, and extremely more. Much is often, again and again, frequently, over and over, repeatedly, time and again. Much is a great deal, heap, lashings, lot, lump, or mass. Much is a mountain, multiplicity, pack, pile, plenty, excess, overage, oversupply, or plethora. It is unlimited and complete favor. It is no lack, only provision favor. It is the kind of favor that can only come from God. And when it's extended to us, we must extend to others.

In essence, Jesus is stating a general principle: the more we have from God, the greater our accountability before God. The more gifts we have, the more God expects us to use those gifts to bless others. The more money we have, the more money God expects us to give. If we have a car and someone needs a ride, God expects us to give that person a ride. If we have two or more cars and someone needs a car, God expects us to give one of those cars away. If we have more shoes in our closet than we can wear and someone doesn't have shoes, God expects us to give them shoes. Get the point? To whom much is given, much is also required.

Finally, favor IS forever. Jeremiah 29:11 reminds us of the following: *"For I know the thoughts that I think toward you, saith the* LORD, *thoughts of peace, and not of evil, to give you an expected end."* God makes His plans for His people, and they are good plans that ultimately bring hope and peace. And God's plans, which are immerses in God's favor, are forever. They don't ever end, terminate, or expire. Forever means forever. Therefore, there is no need for us to ever be afraid or discouraged. We walk in God's complete favor.

Jesus walked in favor. Luke 2:52 notes: *"And Jesus increased in wisdom and stature, and in favour with God and man."* This same favor is available to us. We can have favor with God and with other people. But we must activate our faith to receive it. We must live by faith. We must be confident. We must know that God gives us the same favor Jesus has. Regardless of the circumstances that come into our lives, we must believe God for supernatural favor.

The Principle of Favor. Favor isn't fair. Favor isn't free. And favor is forever.

No Lack, Only Provision!

CHAPTER SIX
The Principle of Faith

Hebrews 11:1

"Now faith is the substance of things hoped for, the evidence of things not seen."

"Any picture firmly held in any mind, in any form, is bound to come forth. That is the great, unchanging Universal Law that, when we cooperate with it intelligently, makes us absolute masters of the conditions and situations in our lives." – John McDonald, The Message of a Master

Faith is a constant outlook of trust towards God, whereby human beings abandon all reliance on their own efforts and put their full confidence in God, God's word and God's promises. The key to greatness with God is faith. The person who truly believes God is great in the eyes of God. Faith must be understood because of its great importance in the life of the believer.

The biblical definition of faith found in Hebrews 11:1 is illuminated in each of the following scriptures or commentaries:

Williams Commentary

> *"Now faith is the assurance of things hoped for, the proof of the reality of the things we cannot see."*

The Amplified Bible

> *Now faith is the assurance (the confirmation, [a]the title deed) of the things [we] hope for, being the proof of things [we] do not see and the conviction of their reality [faith perceiving as real fact what is not revealed to the senses].* – Hebrews 11:1

William Barclay Commentary

> *"Faith means that we are certain of the things we hope for, convinced of the things we do not see"*

Wycliffe Bible Commentary

> *"Faith is trust in the unseen. It is not trust in the unknown, for we may know by faith what we cannot see with the eye."*

Some people suggest that this is blind faith. Hebrews 11:1 however describes faith as a conviction of certainty about what cannot be seen. This kind of faith motivated men and women of faith in the past to live for God and trust God to fulfill God's promises.

True Bible faith is confident obedience to God's Word in spite of circumstances and consequences. This faith operates quite simply. God speaks and we hear God's

Word. We trust God's Word and act on it regardless of what the circumstances are or what the consequences may be. The circumstances may seem impossible and the consequences frightening and unknown, but we must obey God's Word just the same and believe God to do what is right and what is best.

Faith knows what is real. It trusts God completely for everything including our salvation. Romans 8:24 states: *"For we are saved by hope: but hope that is seen is not hope: for what a man seeth, why doth he yet hope for?"* Faith is substance or *"hupostasis"* in the Greek. It means foundation, assurance, guarantee, or title deed. When we have the title deed to something that means we own it. It's ours and we have complete ownership and authority over it. God wants us to have faith in the Word and God's promises based on God's assurance and guarantee that God's Word is sure and God's Word can be trusted. This kind of faith does not require proof up front. It does not require detailed analysis or scientific data before we take action. This kind of faith operates as if we already posses the promise (title deed) because as far as God is concerned, we do!

Faith is experiencing what is real. John 4:42 makes a vivid statement about a real faith based on experience. In the beginning of the fourth chapter, Jesus meets a Samarian woman at the well. After her encounter with Jesus, this woman goes out and tells everyone she can about her experience with Jesus and how it has transformed her life. Because of her testimony, many

Samarians believed Jesus to be the Savior of the world. But by the time we get to John 4:42 we find these words: *"And said unto the woman, Now we believe, not because of thy saying: for we have heard him ourselves, and know that this is indeed the Christ, the Saviour of the world."* In essence, some of the Samarians, after seeking out Jesus for themselves and spending time with Him, had more than just the testimony of another person. These Samarians had a faith based on what is real: a personal relationship with Jesus.

Faith is evidence or *"elegchos"* in the Greek. It is faith based on *"conviction"* and not on speculation or hearsay. If we are convicted about something, or convicted of something, that conviction is based on solid foundational evidence. God is proven.

Finally, faith possesses what is real. Numbers 13:30 is a wonderful example of how we must operate in faith regardless of the situation. *"And Caleb stilled the people before Moses, and said, Let us go up at once, and possess it; for we are well able to overcome it."* Caleb exercised bold faith and spoke with conviction to calm the fears of the Children of Israel who were afraid to posses the land God had already promised was theirs because it had giants in it. Caleb understood faith is an act of the mind and heart. Like Caleb, our hearts and minds must believe what God has said with the conviction that it is true. So we see Caleb saying regardless of the giants and any other obstacles in the land, *"Let us go up and possess it."* Caleb functioned with *"title deed"* faith and moved without fear towards actual possession of the land. And so should we!

The Principle Of Faith. Know what is real. Experience what is real. Possess what is real.

No Lack, Only Provision!

CHAPTER SEVEN
The Principle of Sowing and Reaping

Galatians 6:1-10

¹ "Brethren, if a man be overtaken in a fault, ye which are spiritual, restore such an one in the spirit of meekness; considering thyself, lest thou also be tempted.

² Bear ye one another's burdens, and so fulfil the law of Christ.

³ For if a man think himself to be something, when he is nothing, he deceiveth himself.

⁴ But let every man prove his own work, and then shall he have rejoicing in himself alone, and not in another.

⁵ For every man shall bear his own burden.

⁶ Let him that is taught in the word communicate unto him that teacheth in all good things.

⁷ Be not deceived; God is not mocked: for whatsoever a man soweth, that shall he also reap.

⁸ For he that soweth to his flesh shall of the flesh reap corruption; but he that soweth to the Spirit shall of the Spirit reap life everlasting.

9 And let us not be weary in well doing: for in due season we shall reap, if we faint not.

10 As we have therefore opportunity, let us do good unto all men, especially unto them who are of the household of faith."

"If we are to accomplish anything in a big way, a set definite objective must be established." – John McDonald, The Message of a Master

The Principle of Sowing and Reaping is a critical principle that must be grasped if believers are going to tap into God's unlimited provision. Sowing means to scatter (seed) over land, earth, etc., for growth. To sow is to plant seed for the purpose of growing a crop. When one sows they implant, introduce, or promulgate. Sowing seeks to propagate, extend, or disseminate.

Reaping on the other hand means to cut (wheat, rye, etc.) with a sickle or other instrument or a machine, as in harvest. To reap is to gather or get a return, recompense, or result on what has been sown. In some cases, directly related to the amount of seed planted, one can anticipate reaping large profits.

The Principle of Sowing and Reaping is also called the Law of Sowing and Reaping. The Law of Sowing and Reaping is called a law for a reason. It is a Godly principle and part of a covenant God made with Adam and all of Creation in Genesis 8:22 (our opening scripture): "*While the earth remains, seedtime and harvest, and cold and heat, and summer and winter, and day and night shall not cease.*" So far, the earth has not ceased, which means that the principle of seedtime and harvest reaping and sowing of the Law of Sowing and Reaping remains active and humans can still operate in this principle.

Whenever we obey the laws of God, it takes discipline and faith in the beginning, but in the long run, blessings always follow. When we disobey God, our actions are void of faith and lessons are usually learned the hard way. Sowing or releasing is biblical. The opposite of sowing is hoarding. Hoarding or holding on to anything that should be sown is not biblical. In fact, it's selfish and goes against the very nature of God.

God is the Supreme Giver. God give life. God gives health. God gives restoration. God gives peace. God gives provision. And God give abundantly and in abundance. So, if we are created in God's image and we are imitators of God, we are spiritually born to be givers or sowers. We learn to trust God enough that when God says give, we give.

Bishop David Oyedepo from his work "*Success Systems*" notes:

> "*What the world calls prosperity is how much you have; but in the Kingdom of God, prosperity is determined by how much you give.*"

Charles Capps from his work "*Seedtime and Harvest*" says:

> "*When you see lack and problems in your life,*

speak abundance and peace. That's the seed you are sowing."

Robert Collier explains in *"The Secret of the Ages"*:

"He that sees only plenty, he that expects only plenty, he that works with only plenty in mind, will by his very thought attract that plenty to him."

Galatians chapter 6 gives believers a solid set of foundational and moral ethics to include restoring sinners (6:1); carrying burdens (6:2); evaluating your work (6:3-5); supporting teachers of the Word (6:6); reaping what you sow (6:7-8); and doing good (6:9-10). So let's explore these verses more intently as we seek to gain a deeper understanding of the Principle of Sowing and Reaping.

We are first admonished to bear each other's burdens. Galatians 6:1-5 states: *"Brethren, if a man be overtaken in a fault, ye which are spiritual, restore such an one in the spirit of meekness; considering thyself, lest thou also be tempted. Bear ye one another's burdens, and so fulfil the law of Christ. For if a man think himself to be something, when he is nothing, he deceiveth himself. But let every man prove his own work, and then shall he have rejoicing in himself alone, and not in another. For every man shall bear his own burden."*

My sainted Mother, Mrs. Myrtis L. Adams, who now rests in glory now used to say to my brothers and me, *"Sons, remember, it could be you."* Mama sought to teach us never look down on anyone else or think that we were better than the next person. Their hardship could easily be our hardship. Their challenge could just as easily be our challenge. And if that were the case, we would want someone to have compassion on us, not look down on us or ridicule us because we happened to be experiencing misfortune.

Rather than look down on another person, we are to bear one another's burdens. If we can help the next person, we are admonished to help them. To bear means to carry or share in something that's burdensome. It means to bear or carry a relatively heavy object. But there's an extended definition found in the Greek foundation of the word. To bear or *"bastazo"* means to lift, lift up or raise. In other words, don't just help carry the heavy burden, do what is required to lift to heavy burden from the original burden bearer.

This principle has a second significant importance when it comes to God's leaders, specifically pastors and teachers of the Word. The Apostle Paul makes it clear in this scripture that we are to provide financial support for our ministry leaders. Look at Galatians 6:6; *"Let him that is taught in the word communicate unto him that teacheth in all good things."* It is completely biblical and right to support our pastors and teachers of the Word. While some may disagree, and while unfortunately some pastors and teachers have misused privileges here, this is the system God put in place. It goes all the way back to Levitical Law and the Levitical Priesthood. God's people are supposed to take care of each other beyond just prayers and encouragement. Financial support or *"... communicating unto him that teaches in all good things"* is sound biblical principle. It's at the heart of sowing and reaping.

1 Corinthians 9:9-14 states: *"For it is written in the law of Moses, Thou shalt not muzzle the mouth of the ox that treadeth out the corn. Doth God take care for oxen? Or saith he it altogether for our sakes? For our sakes, no doubt, this is written: that he that ploweth should plow in hope; and that he that thresheth in hope should be partaker of his hope. If we have sown unto you spiritual things, is it a great thing if we shall reap your carnal things? If others be partakers of this power over you, are not we rather? Nevertheless we have not used this power; but suffer all things, lest we should hinder the gospel of Christ. Do ye not know that they which minister about holy things live of the things of the temple? and they which wait at the altar are partakers with the altar? Even so hath the Lord ordained that they which preach the gospel should live of the gospel."*

The English Standard Version reads as follows: *"9 For it is written in the Law of Moses, "You shall not muzzle an ox when it treads out the grain." Is it for oxen that God is concerned? 10 Does he not certainly speak for our sake? It was written for our sake, because the plowman should plow in hope and the thresher thresh in hope of sharing in the crop. 11 If we have sown spiritual things among you, is it too much if we reap material things from you?*

¹² *If others share this rightful claim on you, do not we even more? Nevertheless, we have not made use of this right, but we endure anything rather than put an obstacle in the way of the gospel of Christ.* ¹³ *Do you not know that those who are employed in the temple service get their food from the temple, and those who serve at the altar share in the sacrificial offerings?* ¹⁴ *In the same way, the Lord commanded that those who proclaim the gospel should get their living by the gospel."*

Notice the scripture says *"the Lord commanded that those who proclaim the gospel should get their living by the gospel."* The word *"commanded"* or *"diatasso"* [Greek] means arranged for. God has arranged for those who proclaim (preach and teach) the gospel to obtain our living from the gospel. This is so we can focus our full attention on the Lord's work. Again, it's based on the Levitical Priesthood. The Levites did not receive an inheritance like the other 11 Tribes because the Word of God say in Number 11:20; *"And the LORD said to Aaron, "You shall have no inheritance in their land, neither shall you have any portion among them. I am your portion and your inheritance among the people of Israel."*

Jesus practiced this principle when sending out the 12. Matthew 10:5-10 records these words: *"⁵ These twelve Jesus sent out, instructing them, "Go nowhere among the Gentiles and enter no town of the Samaritans, ⁶ but go rather to the lost sheep of the house of Israel. ⁷ And proclaim as you go, saying, 'The kingdom of heaven is at hand.' ⁸ Heal the sick, raise the dead, cleanse lepers, cast out demons. You received without paying; give without pay. ⁹ Acquire no gold or silver or copper for your belts, ¹⁰ no bag for your journey, or two tunics or sandals or a staff, for the laborer deserves his food."*

Here's the key according to Dr. Mike Murdock: "*What you make happen for others, God will make happen for you.*" So, secondly, don't be selfish. Galatians 6:8 says: "*For he that soweth to his flesh shall of the flesh reap corruption; but he that soweth to the Spirit shall of the Spirit reap life everlasting.*" Being selfish is not a God-given characteristic for any believer. Being selfish is actually operating in the devil's spirit or in the flesh. The Spirit-filled believer is a person that gives. Spirit-filled givers actually seek our opportunities to give because we understand the Principle of Sowing and Reaping. Flowing in this principle is up to us. God doesn't force it. We must willingly sow. And when we do, we can expect to reap a harvest. What we make happen for others will happen for us. What we sow, we will also reap. It's that simple. Here's some further reinforcement of this powerful and pivotal principle:

Mike Murdock states in 101 Wisdom Keys:

"*What you are willing to walk away from determines what God will bring to you.*"

Catherine Ponder explains in Open Your Mind To Prosperity:

"*There is one basic problem in life: congestion. There is one solution: circulation.*"

Let's go back to the Word of God and take a look at 1 Corinthians 6:9; "*9 Know ye not that the unrighteous shall not inherit the kingdom of God? Be not deceived: neither fornicators, nor idolaters, nor adulterers, nor effeminate, nor abusers of themselves with mankind, 10 Nor thieves, nor covetous, nor drunkards, nor revilers, nor extortioners, shall inherit the kingdom of God.11 And such were some of you: but ye are washed, but ye are sanctified, but ye are justified in the name of the Lord Jesus, and by the Spirit of our God.*" Anything that's not righteous before God falls in the category of unrighteousness. Being selfish is not righteous before God. Sowing is righteous because sowing is the very nature of God.

Finally, remember, God is not mocked. Galatians 6:7 is very important and its stern warning is often overlooked as it relates to sowing and reaping from a financial perspective (sowing into God's leader); "*7Be not deceived; God is not mocked: for whatsoever a man soweth, that shall he also reap.*" God will not be mocked or sneered at. God will not have us turn our nose up at the Word of God or God's principles without severe repercussions. What we sow, we will indeed reap.

Paul warns us again in Romans 2:1-6; "*2 Therefore thou art inexcusable, O man, whosoever thou art that judgest: for wherein thou judgest another, thou condemnest thyself; for thou that judgest doest the same things. 2 But we are sure that the judgment of God is according to truth against them which commit such things. ³ And thinkest thou this, O man, that judgest them which do such things, and doest the same, that thou shalt escape the judgment of God? ⁴ Or despisest thou the riches of his goodness and forbearance and longsuffering; not knowing that the goodness of God leadeth thee to repentance? ⁵ But after thy hardness and impenitent heart treasurest up unto thyself wrath against the day of wrath and revelation of the righteous judgment of God; ⁶ Who will render to every man according to his deeds:"*

Can you see why it's critical for us to grasp the Principle of Sowing and Reaping? Jesus gave us the blueprint for the Principle of Sowing and Reaping. Jesus sowed everything when He gave His life for us on Calvary's cross. And because God can be trusted, Jesus rose and reaped a crown in glory!

The Principle Of Sowing and Reaping. Bear each other's burdens. Provide financial support for our ministry leaders. Don't be selfish. Remember, God is not mocked!

CHAPTER EIGHT
The Principle of Generational Wealth

Genesis 25:5-11

⁵ And Abraham gave all that he had unto Isaac.

⁶ But unto the sons of the concubines, which Abraham had, Abraham gave gifts, and sent them away from Isaac his son, while he yet lived, eastward, unto the east country.

⁷ And these are the days of the years of Abraham's life which he lived, an hundred threescore and fifteen years.

⁸ Then Abraham gave up the ghost, and died in a good old age, an old man, and full of years; and was gathered to his people.

⁹ And his sons Isaac and Ishmael buried him in the cave of Machpelah, in the field of Ephron the son of Zohar the Hittite, which is before Mamre;

¹⁰ The field which Abraham purchased of the sons of Heth: there was Abraham buried, and Sarah his wife.

¹¹ And it came to pass after the death of Abraham, that God blessed his son Isaac; and Isaac dwelt by the well Lahai-roi.

"It is your rightful heritage, your birthright, to have anything that you desire, without limit." – John McDonald, The Message of a Master

It is clearly evident from the scriptures that God does not have a problem with riches or money. In fact one of the greatest misinterpretations of the scripture is that *"money is the root of all evil."* 1 Timothy 6:10 actually teaches that the *"LOVE of money is the root of all evil."* Money, in and of itself, is not evil nor is it wrong for Christians to possess it. Money is a tool that is intended as a medium of exchange. Money is to be used to better our world and those around us. Money is to be used to build hospitals, schools, and churches. Money allows us to take care of our daily needs and provides us with many of our comforts.

Money is a taboo subject. Many pastors don't teach about it and many Christians don't want to hear about it. This position against money talk in the church amongst pastors and Christians prevails because of at least two very real reasons. First of all, there have been those in the church, pastors and others entrusted with the churches finances, who have misused, misappropriated, bribed, and stolen the hard-earned donations of God's people for their own personal benefit. Story after story also exists about pastors living lavishly in huge homes, driving high-end luxury cars, and even owning planes and boats while members of those same churches struggle. In some cases, the churches are the pastors source of extravagance. In others, the pastors, who also function as entrepreneurs outside of the church, pave their own way for their lavish lifestyle. Either way, the negative press does not help the church deal responsibly with matters concerning money.

The second, and not as talked about reason why money talk is taboo in the church has to do with the fact that not all churchgoers are generous. There is a broad misconception prevalent in the Body of Christ and outside of the church, that all churches have a surplus of money. I have managed budgets in large and small churches so I have personal observation, experience, and analysis in this area. Whether large or small, roughly 20% of the members carry the church's cost for operations and ministries. 60% give at some level and the remaining 20% don't give at all. Both of the aforementioned issues make money a taboo subject in the church.

But it's important to understand that money is a tool for kingdom building and expanding the reach of the Gospel. Imagine being able to write a check to feed 10,000 needy families. Imagine being able to step up to the plate and say: *"Pastor, we don't need to raise any money, here's a check…go forth with the vision of the church."* That's what money allows us to do! A proper perspective on giving of one's financial means to God's work always results in God rewarding our generosity.

Let's look at some scriptures in this area before we proceed further:

> Proverbs 3:9 – *"Honor the Lord with your wealth and with the firstfruits of all your produce;"*

Proverbs 11:25 – *"Whoever brings blessing will be enriched, and one who waters will himself be watered."*

Luke 6:30 – *"Give to everyone who begs from you, and from one who takes away your goods do not demand them back."*

Luke 6:38 – *"Give, and it will be given to you. Good measure, pressed down, shaken together, running over, will be put into your lap. For with the measure you use it will be measured back to you."*

2 Corinthians 9:7 - *"Each one must give as he has decided in his heart, not reluctantly or under compulsion, for God loves a cheerful giver."*

1 Timothy 6:10 – *"For the love of money is a root of all kinds of evils. It is through this craving that some have wandered away from the faith and pierced themselves with many pangs."*

In this chapter, I want to explore The Principle of Generational Wealth. I want to be very precise and surgical in this chapter because I believe grasping this principle is the difference between living well today and providing the means for generations to come to also live well. Most of us don't experience monetary or generational wealth in our lifetimes because we start from nothing. We are unable to take that nothing and make it into something. Take this into account: the top three ways to become wealthy in America are investments (mainly stocks and real estate), entrepreneurship, and inheritance.

Generational wealth (inheritance) is in the top three.

It is not surprising that God gives us clear examples in scripture of generational wealth being built and passed down. Catherine Ponder's work *"The Millionaires of Genesis: Their Prosperity Secrets for You"* helps us understand that:

> Adam was the first millionaire
> Abraham was the pioneering millionaire
> Melchezidek was the mystical millionaire
> Ishmael was the minority millionaire
> Isaac was the peaceful millionaire
> Jacob was the persistent millionaire
> Joseph was the first billionaire
> Ruth was the first millionairess

At this point it is also instructive to note that generational wealth is not always measured monetarily. Abundance in peace, love, family, friendships are also forms of wealth that can be passed down. But the focus of this chapter isn't peace, love, family, or friendships. The focus of this chapter is tangible assets that can be passed down after those of us reading this chapter have made our earthly transition.

Ponder's work provides us with an awesome historical perspective on Abraham. Genesis 12 begins to describe his history. He is thought of as the Father of the Hebrew people and as a spiritual leader. But Abraham was also a man of vast wealth, which the Bible boldly describes.

Abraham's background gave him both a material understanding and a spiritual understanding of prosperity and how to manifest it in the world.

His life began in the Babylonian city of Ur. The Babylonians were an advanced and prosperous people. They became the richest in their era. They were the first to develop the sound financial principles we regard today to include insurance, savings, home ownership, investments, and systematic tithing. It was into this prosperous, advanced civilization that Abraham was born and spent the first 75 years of his life.

Abraham had the foundational belief system necessary for understanding the Principle of Generational Wealth. Here's some of what Abraham understood and some of the tangible principles we can apply. First, God's plan is for us to produce generational wealth. Genesis 12:1-4 says *"Now the LORD had said unto Abram, Get thee out of thy country, and from thy kindred, and from thy father's house, unto a land that I will shew thee: And I will make of thee a great nation, and I will bless thee, and make thy name great; and thou shalt be a blessing: And I will bless them that bless thee, and curse him that curseth thee: and in thee shall all families of the earth be blessed. So Abram departed, as the LORD had spoken unto him; and Lot went with him: and Abram was seventy and five years old when he departed out of Haran."*

Look closely at Genesis 12:2-3. Do you see what I see? God tells Abraham that he will be a great nation, his name will be great, and he will be a blessing. But it gets even better. God tells Abraham that everyone who blesses him (Abraham) will be blessed and everyone who curses him will be cursed. Now, if you can believe this, it gets even better. The end of Genesis 12:3 is at the heart of what I'm pressing into you who are reading this chapter. *"And in thee shall all families of the earth be blessed."* In essence, Abraham, I decree and declare that you will have generational wealth! Not only will you be blessed, and not only will those who bless you be blessed, everyone who comes after you that is in your family tree will be blessed. What an awesome promise from an Awesome God!

Now, I can hear some of you saying: *"That promise was made to Abraham and his bloodline. That doesn't include me."* You would be correct if we were only interpreting generational wealth from the natural (earthly) perspective and not the biblical (spiritual) perspective. Here's why: Jesus is a direct descendent of Abraham and we who are in Christ are direct descendants of Jesus. That makes us Abraham's seed and therefore heirs to the same promise God gave to Abraham in Genesis 12.

Still need further proof that God's plan is for us to produce generational wealth? Ok, let's take a look at a couple of key scriptures:

Matthew 1:1 places Jesus in Abraham's direct lineage – *"The book of the generation of Jesus Christ, the son of David, the son of Abraham."*

Galatians 3:16 place believers in Jesus' direct lineage

and therefore heirs to Abraham's promise – *"Now to Abraham and his seed were the promises made. He saith not, And to seeds, as of many; but as of one, And to thy seed, which is Christ."*

Our connection to the promises has been secured from Abraham through Jesus Christ. We simply need to accept the plan God has already laid out for all of God's children. Here's an affirmation you can repeat daily: *"I do not depend upon persons or conditions for my prosperity. God is the Source of my supply, and God provides His own amazing channels of prosperity to me now."* (Source: The Complete Personalized Promise Bible on Financial Increase)

The second thing we must be absolutely clear on is the fact that God does not have a problem with us being rich. Genesis 13:1-2 speaks further about Abraham: *"And Abram went up out of Egypt, he, and his wife, and all that he had, and Lot with him, into the south. And Abram was very rich in cattle, in silver, and in gold."* Abram (Abraham) was not just rich he was VERY rich! The word "very" in the context means authentic, bona fide, genuine, sure enough, undoubted, or unquestionably rich.

Abram's mindset was the same one we must have today if we are going to experience all of God's abundance. We must recognize God as our one true Source. We must leave behind limited thoughts and a limited mindset. We must grasp the reality that prosperity in any area of our lives is 98% mental preparation and 2% outer action. It's all about how we think. Even the Proverb writer says *"As a* man [women] thinks in his [her] heart so is he[she]."

Here's another affirmation we can say daily: "*I am now shown new ways of living and new methods of work. I am not confined to the ways and methods of the past.*"

Finally, remember God allows generational wealth that produces expanded territories. Genesis 15:1-6 states: "*15 After these things the word of the LORD came unto Abram in a vision, saying, Fear not, Abram: I am thy shield, and thy exceeding great reward. ² And Abram said, Lord GOD, what wilt thou give me, seeing I go childless, and the steward of my house is this Eliezer of Damascus? ³ And Abram said, Behold, to me thou hast given no seed: and, lo, one born in my house is mine heir. ⁴ And, behold, the word of the LORD came unto him, saying, This shall not be thine heir; but he that shall come forth out of thine own bowels shall be thine heir. ⁵ And he brought him forth abroad, and said, Look now toward heaven, and tell the stars, if thou be able to number them: and he said unto him, So shall thy seed be. ⁶ And he believed in the LORD; and he counted it to him for righteousness.*"

Expanded Territories – this was God's promise to Abram

Fear not – there is truly nothing or no one to fear when God is on our side

Shield – God is our shield; our protection from all enemies and God is ever present

Reward – We are rewarded for our faithfulness just like Abram. We are rewarded for trusting God and having faith in God's promises.

Seed shall outnumber the stars – Herein lies the promise of generational wealth. It begins with us but it multiplies exponentially with our seed ... our children, grandchildren, great-grandchildren and beyond. Our seed shall be so great that they will outnumber the stars. This was God's promise to Abram and it remains God's promise to us.

Abraham believed in the Lord and we must believe in God!

God allows generational wealth that can be passed on to our children and children's children. Genesis 24:1 records how God kept ever promise made to Abraham: *"And Abraham was old, and well stricken in age: and the LORD had blessed Abraham in all things."* God's plan is for us to leave a legacy of generational wealth. Genesis 25:5-11 – *"5 And Abraham gave all that he had unto Isaac. 6 But unto the sons of the concubines, which Abraham had, Abraham gave gifts, and sent them away from Isaac his son, while he yet lived, eastward, unto the east country. 7 And these are the days of the years of Abraham's life which he lived, an hundred threescore and fifteen years. 8 Then Abraham gave up the ghost, and died in a good old age, an old man, and full of years; and was gathered to his people.9 And his sons Isaac and Ishmael buried him in the cave of Machpelah, in the field of Ephron the son of Zohar the Hittite, which is before*

Mamre; ¹⁰ The field which Abraham purchased of the sons of Heth: there was Abraham buried, and Sarah his wife. ¹¹ And it came to pass after the death of Abraham, that God blessed his son Isaac; and Isaac."

I was reminded of a personal example regarding generational wealth during a conversation with my nephew, Ernest Maul, Jr., who we affectionately call "EJ." During a family holiday gathering at his home, the subject of generational wealth came up inadvertently when he began reflecting on the many days that he would come to our home as a college student, and young adult professional after college, to work on our computer. EJ spoke of how that time in the office fueled his passion for entrepreneurship and building a better life for himself, while setting a positive example for his peers and other family members coming behind him.

You might be asking, *"What does EJ's story have to do with generational wealth?"* Here's the correlation: EJ is the son of college educated, highly successful parents. He is the grandson of blue-collar workers who made great sacrifices to provide for their children, his parents. At age 30, he already owns several businesses in multiple states, with plans for further expansion, and his own home. In essence, EJ is the recipient of generational wealth (better standard of living and enhanced opportunities). He has achieved more in his life by age 30 than both his grandparents and parents largely because his grandparents and parents provided the path for him to benefit by the advances each made in their respective generations. In the same manner, when EJ has children, he will continue the blessing of generational wealth by providing an even greater foundation from which his children can build.

The Principle of Generational Wealth. God's plan is for us to produce generational wealth. God does not have a problem with us being rich. God allows generational wealth that produces expanded territories.

CHAPTER NINE
Conclusion

Matthew 6:30-33 (The Message Bible)

"If God gives such attention to the appearance of wildflowers—most of which are never even seen—don't you think he'll attend to you, take pride in you, do his best for you? What I'm trying to do here is to get you to relax, to not be so preoccupied with getting, so you can respond to God's giving. People who don't know God and the way he works fuss over these things, but you know both God and how he works. Steep your life in God-reality, God-initiative, God-provisions. Don't worry about missing out. You'll find all your everyday human concerns will be met."

3 John 2 (The Message Bible)

"I pray for good fortune in everything you do, and for your good health—that your everyday affairs prosper, as well as your soul!"

"Believe me, you can have anything you want – and in abundance – when you learn to tune into the power

within, and infinitely greater power than electricity, a power you have had since the beginning." – John McDonald, The Message of a Master

This has been an amazing book to write. I've thoroughly enjoyed sharing some of the most powerful principles I've learned and continue to apply in my life on a daily basis. No lack, only provision is more than just a mantra. It's more than just a phrase on a t-shirt or ball cap. It's more than just a vision given to me during one of the most challenging times in my life and ministry. No lack, only provision is a movement. And it's here to stay.

I can promise you this: apply these principles in your life and you will experience God's favor and unlimited provision in ways that are pleasantly surprising and unexpectedly awesome. All of God's resources will begin to flow your way. Even in moments of perceived physical lack, there will be no lack because living these principles will always produce provision every time and always on time.

Here's to your life of *No Lack, Only Provision!*

# CHAPTER TEN
30 Days of No Lack, Only Provision Daily Affirmations

Day 1:

Proverbs 10:22 – *"The blessing of the LORD brings wealth, without painful toil for it."*

I am a wealth generating spirit. Money and resources flow freely into my hands and accounts daily. My ideas generate money. My expertise generates money. My gifts and projects generate money. My products generate money. Money flows into my hands daily. I am an excellent steward of what God has entrusted me with. I give freely because I am receiving freely. I live under open heavens.

Day 2:

Luke 4:18-19 – *"The Spirit of the LORD is upon Me, Because He has anointed Me To preach the gospel to the poor; He has sent Me to heal the brokenhearted, To proclaim liberty to the captives And recovery of sight to the blind, To set at liberty those who are oppressed;* *¹⁹To proclaim the acceptable year of the* LORD."

The Spirit of the Lord is upon me. The Spirit of the Lord anoints everything that I think, say, and touch. The Spirit of the Lord orders my footsteps. Therefore, I receive great harvest daily. Harvest in love. Harvest in relationships. Harvest in business. Harvest in finances. Harvest in health and wellbeing. The Spirit of the Lord is upon me. Nothing or no one can block my daily harvest. I'm walking in all of God's favor.

Day 3:

Nehemiah 9:32 – *"Now, therefore, our God, the great, the mighty, and the awesome God, who keeps covenant and steadfast love"*

Great & Mighty! God, You are so awesome. Your word never fails me. You are gracious and merciful to me day by day. Each day brings new promises fulfilled. Thank You for simply being Great & Mighty!

Day 4:

Deuteronomy 8:18 – *"You shall remember the LORD your God, for it is he who gives you power to get wealth, that he may confirm his covenant that he swore to your fathers, as it is this day."*

I am a wealth creator and a wealth magnet. Every thing I touch turns to gold. Every idea I have generates wealth. Wealth flows to me daily. I am a philanthropist because of the wealth that flows my way. The flow is endless, like the waves of the ocean. My accounts are bulging, my storehouses are full, and all of my debts are paid. I have endless surplus. I am a wealth creator and a wealth magnet.

Day 5:

Joshua 1:9 - *"Have I not commanded thee? Be strong and of a good courage; be not afraid, neither be dismayed; for the Lord thy God is with thee withersoever though goest" and of a good courage; be not afraid, neither be dismayed; for the Lord thy God is with thee withersoever though goest"*

I am of good courage. I am physically and mentally alert at all times. The Lord is with me. Everything God has promised me God has delivered. Every one of my enemies has already been defeated.

I am of good courage. I am steadfastly minded, strong, fortified, and hardened for the journey. I enjoy the Lord's specific favor on my life. It belongs to me and me only.

I am of good courage. I am confident and I have already prevailed in every venture I undertake.

I am of good courage. I am bold, stout, solid, and secure. I am of good courage because I am confident that God has me covered at all times.

Day 6:

Joshua 10:22-25 - 22 – "Then said Joshua, Open the mouth of the cave, and bring out those five kings unto *me out of the cave. 23 And they did so, and brought forth those five kings unto him out of the cave, the king of Jerusalem, the king of Hebron, the king of Jarmuth, the king of Lachish, and the king of Eglon. 24 And it came to pass, when they brought out those kings unto Joshua, that Joshua called for all the men of Israel, and said unto the captains of the men of war which went with him, Come near, put your feet upon the necks of these kings. And they came near, and put their feet upon the necks of them. 25 And Joshua said unto them, Fear not, nor be dismayed, be strong and of good courage: for thus shall the Lord do to all your enemies against whom ye fight."*

I am fearless. Every enemy I face today is already defeated. Depression, health challenges, financial challenges, family challenges, employment challenges, broken promises, and shattered dreams are all defeated.

I am fearless. My foot is firmly placed on the neck of all my enemies. I am not dismayed. I am strong. I am courageous. I stand on God's Word. I know God's Word is sure and I know God's Word can be trusted.

Day 7:

Exodus 3:21 – *"And I will give this people **favor** in the sight of the Egyptians; and it shall be, when you go, that you shall not go empty-handed."*

I am experiencing phenomenal growth right now! The entire universe is bent in my favor and I am reaping all of her benefits immediately. Every need is met. Every desire is fulfilled. New mercies. New territories. New growth.

Day 8:

Isaiah 55:10-11 – "*^{10}For as the rain comes down, and the snow from heaven, And do not return there, But water the earth, And make it bring forth and bud, That it may give seed to the sower And bread to the eater, ^{11} So shall My word be that goes forth from My mouth; It shall not return to Me void, But it shall accomplish what I please, And it shall prosper in the thing for which I sent it.*"

God's Word is like the rain and the snow. It comes to replenish the earth. It is a sign that there will always be seed time and harvest. Farmers plant seeds. But the seeds cannot grow without water. The grass will not remain green without water. The trees will not blossom with water. So it is with all creation. Water is the creator and sustainer of life. God's Word is that water. It creates. It sustains. It replenishes. So shall God's Word be now and forever more.

Day 9:

Your Presence is powerful and majestic. It brings light to darkness, hope to the hopeless, peace to those who are without rest, and joy to those who are sad.

Your word says in Luke 6:38 – "*Give, and it shall be given unto you; good measure, pressed down, and shaken together, and running over, shall men give into your bosom. For with the same measure that ye mete withal it shall be measured to you again."*

Today, I speak Luke 6:38 over my life and the life of my family. We are givers. We make tremendous sacrifices in giving of our time, talents, and resources, to include money to everyone who is in need. Therefore, men and women will give into our bosom daily.

The universe is bent toward us in a magnificent manner. Every resource we need is always flowing our way. Favor in money, health, employment, contracts, grants, business opportunities, speaking engagements, houses, and land all flow our way.

We simply need to open our hands and receive. We have no lack, only provision. We receive our provision. In Jesus name, amen.

Day 10:

Philippians 4:19 – *"But my God shall supply all your need according to his riches in glory by Christ Jesus."*

All of my needs are met. My God has released into me abundance. Abundance in spiritual matters. Abundance in physical matters. Abundance in material matters. Abundance in financial matters.

Day 11:

Philippians 2:5 - *"Let this mind be in you, which was also in Christ Jesus:"* (KJV)

The mind of Christ is already in you.

Let your mind go

Let your creativity flow

Let the Christ in you run free

Be all you were created to be

The mind of Christ is already in you!

Day 12:

2 Corinthians 4:7-9 - *"7 But we have this treasure in earthen vessels, that the excellency of the power may be of God, and not of us. 8 We are troubled on every side, yet not distressed; we are perplexed, but not in despair; 9 Persecuted, but not forsaken; cast down, but not destroyed;"* (KJV)

My faith builds with every storm I face in my life. God designed me to weather and overcome the storms. I will not lose heart or hope in the storm. I know that my storms are only temporary. My faith builds with every storm I face. I always have faith in the midst of the storm.

Day 13:

Proverbs 3:1-10 - *"Trust in the Lord – 1 My son, forget not my law; but let thine heart keep my commandments: 2 For length of days, and long life, and peace, shall they add to thee. 3 Let not mercy and truth forsake thee: bind them about thy neck; write them upon the table of thine heart: 4 So shalt thou find favour and good understanding in the sight of God and man. 5 Trust in the LORD with all thine heart; and lean not unto thine own understanding. 6 In all thy ways acknowledge him, and he shall direct thy paths. 7 Be not wise in thine own eyes: fear the LORD, and depart from evil. 8 It shall be health to thy navel, and marrow to thy bones. 9 Honour the LORD with thy substance, and with the firstfruits of all thine increase: 10 So shall thy barns be filled with plenty, and thy presses shall burst out with new wine."*

I trust God with all my heart. I do not lean to my own understanding. I acknowledge God in every way and God directs my path daily. I am a continuous giver. Because I give continuously, I am never without any resource that I need or desire. Money comes to me daily in direct form and via residual streams and investment accounts. My family never wants for anything. My generation is blessed. My children are blessed. My children's children are blessed. My wealth is generational and perpetual. This affirmation I declare and decree daily.

Day 14:

Revelation 5:10 - *"And hast made us unto our God kings and priests: and we shall reign on the earth."*

I am Destined To Reign. I am destined for greatness. I am destined for victory. I am destined for success. I am destined to conquer everywhere are feet tread. I refuse to walk around with my head down I am not defeated. I am not depressed. I am not battered and beaten. Therefore, I will do exactly what the Psalmist instructs. I will lift up head. I am lifted up. The King of Glory shall has come in.

Who is a this King of glory? The Lord strong and mighty. The Lord mighty in battle. I am Destined To Reign.

Day 15:

Numbers 23:19-20 – "*19 God is not a man, that he should lie; neither the son of man, that he should repent: hath he said, and shall he not do it? or hath he spoken, and shall he not make it good. 20 Behold, I have received commandment to bless: and he hath blessed; and I cannot reverse it.*" (KJV)

What God has for me is for me because God keeps all of His promises. God has given me His Command of Blessing. It cannot be reversed. Therefore, I am blessed...PERIOD!

Day 16:

A Prophetic Word:

May God surprise you and meet all of your immediate needs concerning you "THIS WEEK" for caring enough about His people to sacrifice your time to pour into them. May the Almighty God increase you in ways beyond your imagination to set your Ministry apart as one marked for international notoriety, one known for God's Favor, divine intervention and awesome moves of the Spirit, miraculous healing and deliverance in that portion of the vineyard.

May many seek you out, may millions chase you and position you to lend to nations!!! I ask God that as He allows many to come to you, as He's lifted up and draws several to be drawn in, to hear the word and get to know the Lord, the Unchurched, backsliders, those that need a real pure touch from God will know without a doubt the Lord met them there and answered prayer and their hearts desire met. In Jesus Mighty name I have prayed. Amen.

Day 17:

Mark 11:22 *"And Jesus answering, saith to them: Have the faith of God."* -Douay-Rheims 1899 American Edition (DRA)

I have faith. But not just any kind of faith. I have the God kind of faith. I have the faith that God has. I can think like God. I can believe like God. I can speak like God. When I believe God, and I speak what God speaks, God has a way of making the miraculous happen. God does this simply because He is God and I am exercising the God kind of faith. I have the God kind of faith. I am created in God's image. I have everything that God has. Just as the Psalmist proclaims in Psalm 82:6, I am a little god.

Day 18:

2 Kings 6:17 – *"And Elisha prayed, and said, Lord, I pray thee, open his eyes, that he may see. And the Lord opened the eyes of the young man; and he saw: and, behold, the mountain was full of horses and chariots of fire round about Elisha."*

Visualization is the practice and discipline of creating positive images in our minds. It is a mental technique that uses the imagination and relies on faith to overcome our fears and make visions and dreams come true.

When I use it in the right way, visualization will improve my live and attract success and prosperity. It is a power that will alter my environment and circumstances. It causes events to happen and attracts money, possessions, work, people and love into my life. Visualization uses the power of my mind, and is the power behind all of my success.

If I can visualize it, I can have it. If I can see it, I can have it. I have to see it before it happens. I have see it while God is working it out.

Day 19:

I will trust in the Lord.

Psalm 16:1- *"Preserve me, O God: for in thee do I put my trust."*

Psalm 37:3 – *"Trust in the Lord, and do good; so shalt thou dwell in the land, and verily thou shalt be fed."*

Psalm 62:8 – *"Trust in him at all times; ye people, pour out your heart before him: God is a refuge for us. Selah."*

Psalm 91:2 – *"I will say of the Lord, He is my refuge and my fortress: my God; in Him will I trust."*

Proverbs 3:5-6 – *"Trust in the Lord with all thine heart; and lean not unto thine own understanding. In all thy ways acknowledge Him, and He shall direct thy paths."*

Day 20:

Psalm 24: *"The earth is the Lord's, and the fullness thereof."*

The law of abundance says there is more than enough for everyone. Abundance exists and is thriving, not only in the physical world we see with our five human senses, but even beyond in the unseen, metaphysical realm. It's thriving in the supernatural. The law of abundance is without limitations. God is not limited. The law of abundance knows no lack.

Day 21:

Matthew 18:18 – *"Verily I say unto you, Whatsoever ye shall bind on earth shall be bound in heaven: and whatsoever ye shall loose on earth shall be loosed in heaven."*

I have the keys to the Kingdom. Whatever I bind on earth, will be bound in Heaven. And whatever I loose on earth, will be loosed in Heaven. I refuse to sit around idle. I use the keys daily to unlock my destiny and walk in my God-ordained purpose.

Day 22:

Galatians 3:29 – *"And if ye be Christ's, then are ye*

Abraham's seed, and heirs according to the promise."

I am Abraham's seed. Therefore, I am Abraham's heir. The promise of God made to Abraham in Genesis 12 also belongs to me. God made Abraham a great nation. I too am a great nation. My seed, like Abraham, is also innumerable. My seed is blessed forever and will generate after its kind for generations to come.

Day 23:

Genesis 30:43 – *"And the man increased exceedingly, and had much cattle, and maidservants, and menservants, and camels, and asses."*

I follow God therefore I expect increase. I am blessed like Jacob who experienced exceeding increase. God lacks for nothing so I lack for nothing. God rejoices in my prosperity therefore I declare, decree, and walk daily in total abundance.

Day 24:

Exodus 4:2-5 - *And the Lord said unto him, "What is that in thine hand?" And he said, "A rod. "And He said, "Cast it on the ground." And he cast it on the ground, and it became a serpent; and Moses fled from before it. And the Lord said unto Moses, "Put forth thine hand, and take it by the tail." And he put forth his hand, and caught it, and it became a rod in his hand: "That they may believe that the Lord God of their fathers, the God of Abraham, the God of Isaac,* and the God of Jacob, hath appeared unto thee." (KJV)

God points me to the miracle of the rod daily. God points me to the miracle of the rod so that like Moses, my testimony will be: *"That they may believe that the Lord has appeared unto thee."* In essence, what I bring in my hand is all I will need to prove that I AM with me. The miracle I need is in my hand. The answer to the problem I need to solve is in my hand. My hands are blessed and everything I touch prospers.

Day 25:

Jeremiah 29:11 – *"For I know the plans I have for you, declares the LORD, plans for welfare and not for evil, to give you a future and a hope."* (ESV)

The two most important days in your life are the day you are born and the day you find out why God has a plan for your life. God plan is to prosper you, not harm you. God's plan is your future. Tap into God's plan. Live the life you were born to live.

Day 26:

John 3:16 – *"For God so loved the world, that he gave his only begotten Son, that whosoever believeth in him should not perish, but have everlasting life."*

God thought I was worth saving. God's son, Jesus Christ, sacrificed His life so that I would not perish. I can life my life to the fullest here on earth because of Christ's sacrifice. I have the promise of eternal life because of

Christ's sacrifice. God thought I was worth saving.

Day 27:

From this point forward, move only in the direction of your true net worth, and not in the direction of the value others have assigned to you, especially if it's a lesser value.

Day 28:

Ephesians 1:7-8 – "*7 In whom we have redemption through his blood, the forgiveness of sins, according to the riches of his grace; 8 Wherein he hath abounded toward us in all wisdom and prudence;*"

God has given us wisdom and understanding. Exercise it today and be blessed beyond expectation.

Day 29:

Deuteronomy 1:30 – "*30 The LORD your God which goeth before you, he shall fight for you, according to all that he did for you in Egypt before your eyes;*"

Let the Lord fight your battles.

Day 30:

Isaiah 9:6-7 – "*6 For unto us a child is born, unto us a son is given: And the government shall be upon his shoulder: And his name shall be called Wonderful, Counsellor, The mighty God, The everlasting Father, The Prince of Peace. 7 Of the increase of his government and peace there shall be no end, Upon the throne of David, and upon his kingdom, To order it, and to establish it with judgment and with justice From henceforth even for ever. The zeal of the LORD of hosts will perform this."*

Whatever God has promised you, God has the power to bring to pass. Get in touch with God's promises to you. Remember, the zeal of the Lord will accomplish everything He has promised.

CHAPTER ELEVEN

No Lack, Only Provision
30 Days of Scriptures

Day 1:

Genesis 1:28-31 (NKJV)

²⁸ Then God blessed them, and God said to them, "Be fruitful and multiply; fill the earth and subdue it; have dominion over the fish of the sea, over the birds of the air, and over every living thing that moves on the earth." ²⁹ And God said, "See, I have given you every herb that yields seed which is on the face of all the earth, and every tree whose fruit yields seed; to you it shall be for food. ³⁰ Also, to every beast of the earth, to every bird of the air, and to everything that creeps on the earth, in which there is life, I have given every green herb for food"; and it was so. ³¹ Then God saw everything that He had made, and indeed it was very good. So the evening and the morning were the sixth day.

Day 2:

Deuteronomy 28:1-13 (NKJV)

¹ Now it shall come to pass, if you diligently obey the voice of the LORD your God, to observe carefully all His commandments which I command you today, that the LORD your God will set you high above all nations of the earth. ² And all these blessings shall come upon you and overtake you, because you obey the voice of the LORD your God: ³ "Blessed shall you be in the city, and blessed shall you be in the country. ⁴ "Blessed shall be the fruit of your body, the produce of your ground and the increase of your herds, the increase of your cattle and the offspring of your flocks. ⁵ "Blessed shall be your basket and your kneading bowl. ⁶ "Blessed shall you be when you come in, and blessed shall you be when you go out. ⁷ "The LORD will cause your enemies who rise against you to be defeated before your face; they shall come out against you one way and flee before you seven ways. ⁸ "The LORD will command the blessing on you in your storehouses and in all to which you set your hand, and He will bless you in the land which the LORD your God is giving you. ⁹ "The LORD will establish you as a holy people to Himself, just as He has sworn to you, if you keep the commandments of the LORD your God and walk in His ways. ¹⁰ Then all peoples of the earth shall see that you are called by the name of the LORD, and they shall be afraid of you. ¹¹ And the LORD will grant you plenty of goods, in the fruit of your body, in the increase of your livestock, and in the produce of your ground, in the land of which the LORD swore to your fathers to give you. ¹² The LORD will open to you His good treasure, the heavens, to give the rain to your land in its season, and to bless all the work of your hand. You shall lend to many nations, but you shall not borrow. ¹³ And the LORD will make you the head and not the tail; you shall be above only, and not be beneath, if you heed the commandments of the LORD your God, which I command you today, and are careful to observe them.

Day 3:

Psalm 1:3 (NKJV)

³ He shall be like a tree Planted by the rivers of water, That brings forth its fruit in its season, Whose leaf also shall not wither; And whatever he does shall prosper.

Day 4:

Psalm 23:1 (NKJV)

¹ The LORD is my shepherd; I shall not want.

Day 5:

Psalm 35:27 (NKJV)

27 Let them shout for joy and be glad, Who favor my righteous cause; And let them say continually, "Let the Lord be magnified, Who has pleasure in the prosperity of His servant."

Day 6:

Proverbs 3:9-10 (NKJV)

9 Honor the Lord with your possessions, And with the firstfruits of all your increase; 10 So your barns will be

filled with plenty, And your vats will overflow with new wine.

Day 7:

Proverbs 11:24-25 (NKJV)

24 There is one who scatters, yet increases more; And there is one who withholds more than is right, But it leads to poverty. 25 The generous soul will be made rich, And he who waters will also be watered himself.

Day 8:

Proverbs 28:27 (NKJV)

27 He who gives to the poor will not lack, But he who hides his eyes will have many curses.

Day 9:

Jeremiah 29:11

11 For I know the thoughts that I think toward you, saith the LORD, thoughts of peace, and not of evil, to give you an expected end. [1]

Day 10:

Matthew 6:25 (NKJV)

25 Therefore I say to you, do not worry about your life, what you will eat or what you will drink; nor about your

---

[1] *The Holy Bible: King James Version.* (2009). (Electronic Edition of the 1900 Authorized Version., Je 29:11). Bellingham, WA: Logos Research Systems, Inc.

body, what you will put on. Is not life more than food and the body more than clothing?

Day 11:

Matthew 6:30-34 (NKJV)

30 Now if God so clothes the grass of the field, which today is, and tomorrow is thrown into the oven, will He not much more clothe you, O you of little faith? 31 "Therefore do not worry, saying, 'What shall we eat?' or 'What shall we drink?' or 'What shall we wear?' 32 For after all these things the Gentiles seek. For your heavenly Father knows that you need all these things. 33 But seek first the kingdom of God and His righteousness, and all these things shall be added to you. 34 Therefore do not worry about tomorrow, for tomorrow will worry about its own things. Sufficient for the day is its own trouble.

Day 12:

Matthew 17:20 (NKJV)

20 So Jesus said to them, "Because of your unbelief; for assuredly, I say to you, if you have faith as a mustard seed, you will say to this mountain, 'Move from here to there,' and it will move; and nothing will be impossible for you.

Day 13:

Mark 11:22-24 (NKJV)

22 So Jesus answered and said to them, "Have faith in God. 23 For assuredly, I say to you, whoever says to this mountain, 'Be removed and be cast into the sea,' and does not doubt in his heart, but believes that those things he says will be done, he will have whatever he says. ²⁴ Therefore I say to you, whatever things you ask when you pray, believe that you receive them, and you will have them.

Day 14:

John 16:13 (NKJV)

¹³ However, when He, the Spirit of truth, has come, He will guide you into all truth; for He will not speak on His own authority, but whatever He hears He will speak; and He will tell you things to come.

Day 15:

Romans 5:17 (NKJV)

¹⁷ For if by the one man's offense death reigned through the one, much more those who receive abundance of grace and of the gift of righteousness will reign in life through the One, Jesus Christ.

Day 16:

1 Corinthians 2:9

⁹ But as it is written: "Eye has not seen, nor ear heard, Nor have entered into the heart of man The things which God has prepared for those who love Him."

Day 17:

2 Corinthians 6:10

10 as sorrowful, yet always rejoicing; as poor, yet making many rich; as having nothing, and yet possessing all things.

Day 18:

Galatians 3:14

14 that the blessing of Abraham might come upon the Gentiles in Christ Jesus, that we might receive the promise of the Spirit through faith.

Day 19:

Galatians 6:3-9

3 For if anyone thinks himself to be something, when he is nothing, he deceives himself. 4 But let each one examine his own work, and then he will have rejoicing in himself alone, and not in another. 5 For each one shall bear his own load.

6 Let him who is taught the word share in all good things with him who teaches. 7 Do not be deceived, God is not mocked; for whatever a man sows, that he will also reap. 8 For he who sows to his flesh will of the flesh reap corruption, but he who sows to the Spirit will of the Spirit reap everlasting life. 9 And let us not grow weary while doing good, for in due season we shall reap if we do not lose heart.

Day 20:

Philippians 4:19

19 And my God shall supply all your need according to His riches in glory by Christ Jesus.

Day 21:

Colossians 1:1-3

3 We give thanks to the God and Father of our Lord Jesus Christ, praying always for you, 4 since we heard of your faith in Christ Jesus and of your love for all the saints; 5 because of the hope which is laid up for you in heaven, of which you heard before in the word of the truth of the gospel,

Day 22:

1 Thessolonians 3:11-12

11 Now may our God and Father Himself, and our Lord Jesus Christ, direct our way to you. 12 And may the Lord make you increase and abound in love to one another and to all, just as we do to you, 13 so that He may establish your hearts blameless in holiness before our God and Father at the coming of our Lord Jesus Christ with all His saints.

Day 23:

Hebrews 10:23

23 Let us hold fast the confession of our hope without wavering, for He who promised is faithful.

Day 24:

James 1:5-8

⁵ If any of you lacks wisdom, let him ask of God, who gives to all liberally and without reproach, and it will be given to him. ⁶ But let him ask in faith, with no doubting, for he who doubts is like a wave of the sea driven and tossed by the wind. ⁷ For let not that man suppose that he will receive anything from the Lord; ⁸ he is a double-minded man, unstable in all his ways.

Day 25:

1 John 4:4

⁴ You are of God, little children, and have overcome them, because He who is in you is greater than he who is in the world.

Day 26:

1 John 5:13-15

¹³ These things have I written unto you that believe on the name of the Son of God; that ye may know that ye have eternal life, and that ye may believe on the name of the Son of God. ¹⁴ And this is the confidence that we have in him, that, if we ask any thing according to his will, he heareth us: ¹⁵ And if we know that he hear us, whatsoever we ask, we know that we have the petitions that we desired of him.

Day 27:

3 John 2

² Beloved, I ᶜwish above all things that thou mayest prosper and be in health, even as thy soul prospereth.

Day 28:

Revelation 4:10-11

¹⁰ The four and twenty elders fall down before him that sat on the throne, and worship him that liveth for ever and ever, and cast their crowns before the throne, saying, ¹¹ Thou art worthy, O Lord, to receive glory and ʰhonour and power: for thou hast created all things, and for thy pleasure they are and were created.

Day 29:

Revelation 12:11

¹¹ And they overcame him by the blood of the Lamb and by the word of their testimony, and they did not love their lives to the death.

Day 30:

Genesis 8:22

²² ᵗWhile the earth remaineth, seedtime and harvest, and cold and heat, and summer and winter, and day and night shall not cease.

CHAPTER TWELVE
Supporting Quotes

"*You can do whatever you put your mind to.*" – Mrs. Myrtis L. Adams, Mama

"*God keeps things before us until we get the lesson and change our approach toward His perfect will for our lives.*" – Greta E. Adams, Social Worker, Consultant, Wife, Mother, and Grandmother

"*Unleash your potential and awaken the entrepreneurial giant in you.*" – Anthony Robbins, Coach, Chairman, and New York Times Best Selling Author

"*Dream big. Work Hard. Someone has to be the best. Why not you?*" – John C. Maxwell, Leadership Expert, Speaker, Best-Selling Author, and Founder of Equip and the John Maxwell Co.

"*Train your mind to serve you. How we live our lives is a result of the story we believe about ourselves. We have to consciously create and recreate our thinking with seminars, reading and the goals we set. It's important *that we develop an achievement driven mindset."* – Les Brown, Author and Motivational Speaker

"Write a personal mission statement that tells you what your purpose is and what values are going to guide your journey. It should be a personal, compelling vision so you know where you're trying to head and what you want to leave." – Ken Blanchard, Author, Speaker, Coach, and Member of Amazon's Hall of Fame

"Focus on your successes, not your failures. Keep a victory box. Replace negative self-talk with positive affirmations." – Jack Canfield, Co-Author of the Chicken Soup for the Soul series

"When you change the way you look at things, the things you look at change." – Wayne Dyer, Ph.D., Author and World-Renowned Radio Host

"You need to set aside time for reflection, from which you can evaluate, out of all the busyness that has cluttered your life, what the most fulfilling activities are in your life. What makes your adrenaline race? What do you really care about that you would do for free?" – Bishop T. D. Jakes, Pastor, The Potter's House and Best-Selling Author

"You've got to take care of who you are first. Money comes from your efforts to go out and work, save, and invest – all of that. So money really starts with you, and without you, there is no money, and without money, there are no things. You've got to take care of you, and the way you take care of yourself is by having money.

And when you have enough money, you can buy the things you want." – Suze Orman, Financial Expert, Author, and Syndicated Radio Host

"It doesn't matter how far you might rise. At some point, you are bound to stumble. If you are constantly pushing yourself higher and higher, the law of averages predicts that will will at some point fall. And when you do, I want you to remember this:: There is no such thing as failure. Failure is just life trying to move you in another direction." – Oprah Winfrey, Named the 14th amongst the World's Most Powerful Women by Forbes

"Every time you write your goals, you program them deeper into your subconscious, and you activate the Law of Attraction. You start to attract people of a certain status into your life. You start to see possibilities you haven't seen before. You start to hear ideas you wouldn't have noticed before. It's an amazing thing." – Brian Tracey, Entrepreneur, Author and Personal Development Expert.

"Success is nothing more than a few simple disciplines practiced every day." – Jim Rohn, Success Leader and Mentor To The Masters

"Optimism is the faith that leads to achievement; Nothing can be done without hope." – Helen Keller, Author and Political Activist

"Man's greatness consists in his ability to do and the proper application of his powers to things needful to be done." – Frederick Douglass, Abolitionist, Orator, Writer, and Statesman

"*You don't win once in while; you don't do things right once in a while; you do them right all of the time. Winning is a habit.*" – Vince Lombardi, Legendary Head Coach of the Green Bay Packers

"*I visualize. I think of what short-term and long-term steps are needed to accomplish my goals and under what timeframe. Once I have a sense of the pacing required, I ensure that I achieve at least one thing that will move me toward these goals each day.*" – Tiffanny Pham, Founder and CEO of MOGUL

"*Believing. If you do not believe, then you will never achieve. It is quite simple actually. Even if your goal is a long shot, you have to believe at least enough to fuel your efforts. From there it becomes all about hard work and hustle.*" – Lauren Imparato, Founder and CEO of I.AM.YOU

"*Not only will you be healthier if you take care of yourself, you'll be more productive.*" – Emma Johnson, Journalist, Blogger, and Radio Host

"*Setting a goal is not the main thing. It is deciding how you will go about achieving it and staying with that plan.*" – Tom Landry, Legendary Head Coach of the Dallas Cowboys

"*In many cases doing something new means going up against powerful incumbents that will do whatever it takes to keep your idea down."* – Travis Kalanick, Co-Founder and CEO of Uber

"First they think you're crazy. Then they fight you. Then all of a sudden you change the world." – Elizabeth Holmes, Founder and CEO of Therenos

"The size of the goal doesn't matter. What matters is having the desire to improve yourself, push yourself to new limits and adopt the right mindset to make it happen." – James Lawrence, Completed 50 Ironman Races in 50 Days

"It's important that you keep busy. I tell my kids: Every time you hit the floor in the morning, you better hit it with, "On your mark, get set," like a track runner. Every time you hit the floor, you gotta have something that you're working on. Otherwise you're just going to melt away and be nothing." – George Foreman, Former Heavyweight Boxing Champion

"Don't go into the new year holding a grudge from last year. Leave the hurt and disappointments behind." – Joel Osteen, Pastor and Best-Selling Author

"Wait patiently. I believe there is probably no greater evidence of faith than patient waiting. Our confession of faith may be good evidence. There may be all kinds of evidence. But there is no greater evidence of our faith than patiently waiting on God in the midst of circumstances that scream at you saying, "You aren't going to get it!" – Joyce Meyer, Christian Author and Speaker

"Worry reduces your faith and ruins your perspective on life. Your life is more than survival. You were designed by God to thrive." – Bryan Hudson, Pastor, Author, and Community Leader

"Love is both transformational and creative. It is no surprise that the Christian Faith tradition teaches that God IS Love. One of the most foundational truths of life is this: a Person becomes like that which they Love. For what you love is what you'll become. It's true in relationships, it's true in business, it's true in life. Show me what you really love and I'll show you who you really are." - Rev. Nicolas V. O'Rourke

Asst. Pastor of Worship & Liturgical Arts, Living Water UCC, Founding Member of SpiritualityMATTERS

"If you don't like something, change it. If you can't change it, change your attitude." – Maya Angelou, Author, Poet and Civil Rights Activist

No Lack Only Provision Journal Page
The Principle of Dominion

Use this space to express how you will apply this principle daily

No Lack Only Provision Journal Page
The Principle of Seed Time and Harvest

Use this space to express how you will apply this principle daily

No Lack Only Provision Journal Page
The Principle of Departure

Use this space to express how you will apply this principle daily

_____
_____
_____
_____
_____
_____
_____
_____
_____
_____
_____
_____
_____
_____
_____
_____
_____
_____
_____
_____
_____

No Lack Only Provision Journal Page
The Principle of Fearlessness

Use this space to express how you will apply this principle daily

---

No Lack Only Provision Journal Page
The Principle of Favor

Use this space to express how you will apply this principle daily

_____
_____
_____
_____
_____
_____
_____
_____
_____
_____
_____
_____
_____
_____
_____
_____
_____
_____
_____
_____
_____
_____

No Lack Only Provision Journal Page
The Principle of Faith

Use this space to express how you will apply this principle daily

No Lack Only Provision Journal Page
The Principle of Sowing and Reaping

Use this space to express how you will apply this principle daily

_____
_____
_____
_____
_____
_____
_____
_____
_____
_____
_____
_____
_____
_____
_____
_____
_____
_____
_____
_____
_____
_____
_____
_____

No Lack Only Provision Journal Page
The Principle of Generational Wealth
Use this space to express how you will apply this principle daily

_____

_____

_____

_____

_____

_____

_____

_____

_____

_____

_____

_____

_____

_____

_____

_____

_____

_____

_____

_____

_____

_____

_____

Bibliography/Additional Resources

Unless otherwise indicated, all Scripture quotations are taken from the King James Version of The Holy Bible.

Adam Clarke's Commentary on the Whole Bible

Albert Barnes' Commentary on the Whole Bible

Bardwick, Judith M. (1995). *Danger in the Comfort Zone: From Boardroom to Mailroom--how to Break the Entitlement Habit That's Killing American Business.* AMACOM Div American Mgmt Assn. ISBN 978-0-8144-7886-8

Jamieson, R., Fausset, A. R., Fausset, A. R., Brown, D., & Brown, D. *A Commentary, Critical and Explanatory, on the Old and New Testaments.* Oak Harbor, WA: Logos Research Systems, Inc. 1997.

Capps, Charles. *Your Spiritual Authority.* England, AR. Capps Publishing. 1980.

McDonald, John. *The Message of a Master.* Novato, CA. New World Library. 1993.

Ponder, Catherine. *The Millionaires of Genesis: Their Prosperity Secrets for You.* Camarillo, CA. DeVorss & Company Publising. 1976.

Riddle, James. *The Complete Personalized Promise Bible on Financial Increase.* Tulsa, OK. Harrison House. 2006.

The Teacher's Bible Commentary

Walvoord, J. F., Zuck, R. B., & Dallas Theological Seminary. The Bible Knowledge Commentary: An exposition of the Scriptures. Wheaton, IL: Victor Books. 1983.

About The Author

The Reverend Dr. Preston T. Adams, III—pastor, philanthropist, certified leadership development coach and human development expert—was born and raised in Chicago, Illinois. He is the oldest of four sons born to Priestley T. and Myrtis L. Adams, both of whom are deceased.

Dr. Adams, a lifelong learner, has earned three university/seminary degrees. Dr. Adams earned a Bachelor of Science Degree in Business Administration/Computer Science from Central State University, Wilberforce, Ohio (1982), and Masters and Doctor of Divinity Degrees from Christian Theological Seminary (Indianapolis, Indiana, 1996 and 2005 respectively). Dr. Adams completed his Doctor of Ministry Degree with a 3.9 GPA and in a record two-year timeframe!

Dr. Adams is the founding and senior pastor of Amazing Grace Christian Church (Disciples of Christ). Amazing Grace launched in September 2010 on the northeast side of Indianapolis. Amazing Grace shares the love of Jesus Christ by encouraging, equipping and empowering all of God's people to go and make disciples. Amazing Grace embodies the love of Jesus Christ by its focus on *Word, Worship,* and *Witness*. This represents one of the greatest moves of God in Dr. Adams' life.

Dr. Adams is the devoted husband of one wife for over 31 years and the father of three daughters. He and his wife are also blessed with one beautiful granddaughter.

No Lack, Only Provision!

For Additional Publications by Dr. Adams, Please Contact:

PTA Ministries, Inc.
9801 Fall Creek Road, Suite 325
Indianapolis, IN 46256

Or, visit Dr. Adams' websites:
www.prestonadams.com
www.comemeetgrace.org

Made in the USA
Charleston, SC
29 February 2016